What's in This Book?

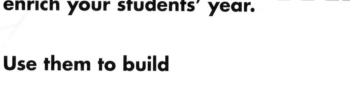

Celebrate each season

of the year with

art activities that will

enrich your students' year.

Use them to build

student-centered bulletin

boards or as motivators

for language and writing

activities.

SPRING

WINTERWITHDRAWN

FALL

SUMMER

Getting Ready for Arts and Crafts

In addition to construction paper in a variety of colors, the projects in this book use other easy-to-obtain materials.

- hole punch
- scissors
- pinking shears
- craft knife (for adult use only)
- stapler
- tempera paint
- shallow dishes

- toothbrushes
- sponges
- clear contact paper or laminate
- newspaper
- waxed paper
- tissue paper

- roving, yarn, and cord
- tongue depressors and/or craft sticks
- straws
- paper fasteners and paper clips
- pipe cleaners

- colored pencils
- crayons
- ink pads
- clear plastic fishing line
- fabric
- ribbon and lace

- cotton balls
- glitter
- foil star stickers
- beans and seeds
- beads
- bells

- paper towels
- paper lunch bags
- glue
- double-stick tape
- marking pens
- gel pens

2

Contents

A Tree for Fall

This colorful fall free uses an ordinary paper bag to create a project with depth and texture.

MATERIALS

- 9" x 12" (23 x 30.5 cm) black construction paper for the background
- 1" x 5" (2.5 x 12.5 cm) red, orange, and yellow construction paper for the leaves
- 4" (10 cm) square of green construction paper for the grass
- 12" x 13" (30.5 x 33 cm) yellow construction paper for the frame
- ½" x 2" (1 x 5 cm) black construction paper strips for the lettering
- brown paper bag for the trunk
- glue
- scissors

STEPS TO FOLLOW

1. Crumple up the paper bag. Flatten out the crinkles and cut three slits as shown.

2. Round the top two corners of the green paper. Glue it to the bottom of the black paper.

3. Glue the trunk to the black construction paper. Allow some branches to buckle or twist.

4. Tear the colored paper strips into pieces. Dip the corner of each piece into a glue puddle and add to the tree. Overlap as you glue.

5. Glue the finished tree to the yellow paper backing.

6. Cut the black strips to spell out the word FALL along the side. Glue the letters in place.

This appealing project is enhanced by written descriptions.

Sponge-Print Trees

MATERIALS

- labels on the following page, reproduced for each student

- 8" x 18" (20 x 45.5 cm) blue construction paper

- 12" x 18" (30.5 x 45.5 cm) black construction paper for the background

- tempera paint: brown, green, and pink

- sponges cut into small rectangular pieces

- apple wedges

- paper towels

- shallow dishes

- cotton balls

- pencils with new erasers

- scissors

- glue

STEPS TO FOLLOW

1. Fold the blue paper into quarters. Open and press flat.

2. Pour the paint into shallow dishes. Dip a sponge into the brown paint. Blot lightly on a paper towel to remove the excess paint before pressing it onto the blue paper.

3. Create four tree trunks—one for each season of the year. Let the paint dry thoroughly.

4. Now customize the trees for each season: fall—bare branches; winter—pulled strips of cotton; spring—colorful blossoms printed with pencil erasers dipped in pink paint; summer—green leaves printed with the ends of apple wedges and green paint.

5. Glue the blue paper to the black background sheet.

6. Cut out the seasonal labels. Add a sentence to each one, describing the tree during that season. Glue the labels below the appropriate trees.

Art for All Seasons • EMC 2001 • ©2004 by Evan-Moor Corp.

This lesson is a natural accompaniment to a unit on apples. One display idea is to create a border for a bulletin board featuring student writings on apples.

MATERIALS

- 6" (15 cm) square of black construction paper for the background
- 5" (12.5 cm) square of red or yellow construction paper
- 4" (10 cm) square of white construction paper
- scraps of green construction paper for the stem and leaf
- black beans
- scissors
- glue

Apple Art

STEPS TO FOLLOW

1. Fold the red or yellow paper in half. Cut one-half of an apple shape on the fold.

2. Fold and cut the white paper in the same shape.

3. Glue the white shape to the colored shape.

4. Cut a stem and a leaf from the green paper.

5. Arrange all the pieces on the black square. Glue the pieces down.

6. Glue on black beans to represent seeds.

My Scarecrow

MATERIALS

- patterns on the following page, reproduced for each student
- 4" x 11" (10 x 28 cm) white construction paper for the scarecrow
- 6" x 9" (15 x 23 cm) brown construction paper for the base
- 8" x 10" (20 x 25.5 cm) green construction paper for the frame
- scraps of green paper
- tongue depressor
- scissors
- glue
- crayons, marking pens, or colored pencils

STEPS TO FOLLOW

1. Color and cut out the pattern pieces.

2. Follow the folding instructions.

3. Fold the white construction paper in half. Glue the scarecrow pattern to it, matching up the center fold. Trim off the excess white paper along each side. Fold under the extra white paper on the bottom to create flaps for gluing.

4. Use glue to secure the tongue depressor in the center fold.

5. Glue on the scarecrow's head and the bird on his arm. Glue the two bottom flaps to the brown construction paper base.

6. Glue the brown paper to the green construction paper.

7. Cut green paper scraps to add sprouting plants around the scarecrow's feet.

Art for All Seasons • EMC 2001 • ©2004 by Evan-Moor Corp.

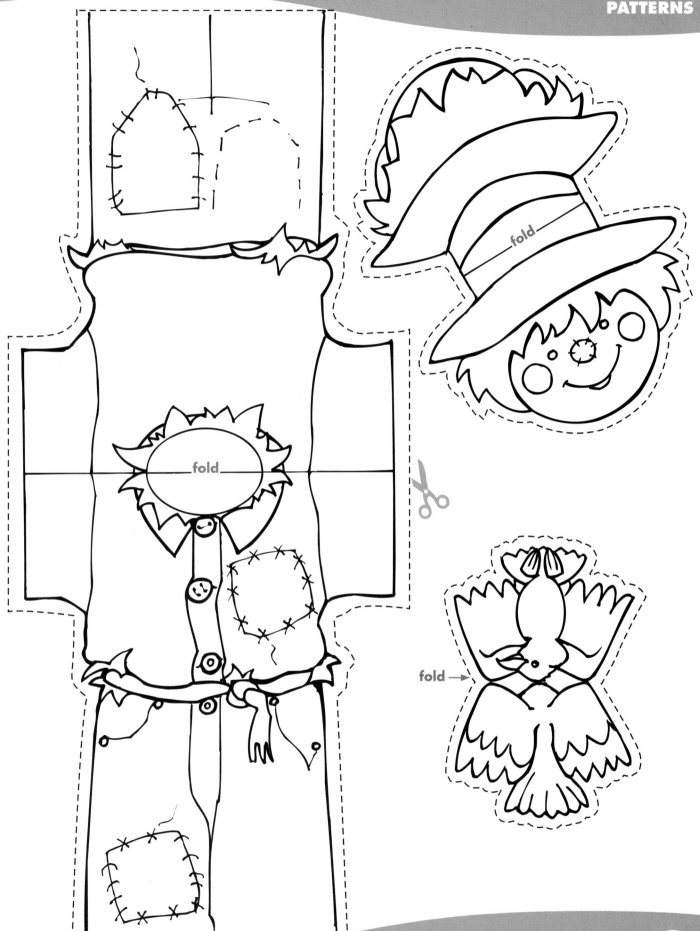

Watch the Seasons Turn

Save these completed projects and bring them out as the seasons change to stimulate discussion and writing about seasonal changes.

MATERIALS

- template and pattern on the following 2 pages
- 7" x 10" (18 x 25 cm) black construction paper for the frame
- 9" x 12" (23 x 30.5 cm) white construction paper
- 6" (15 cm) square of white construction paper for the wheel
- green construction paper scraps
- white tissue paper
- paper fastener
- crayons, marking pens, or colored pencils
- scissors
- craft knife
- pencil
- glue

STEPS TO FOLLOW

1. Fold the larger white construction paper in half.

2. Use the template to locate the area to be cut out. Trace around the triangular opening in pencil and then cut on the pencil line with a craft knife.

3. Using the template as a guide, mark dots that indicate where to insert the paper fastener through the center of the wheel and then through the folded form. Insert the fastener and close the form.

4. Sketch a tree trunk on the front of the form. It should branch around the triangular opening. Add other details to the background.

5. Now sketch the bare branches of a winter tree inside the triangular window. Keep turning the wheel and drawing until you have drawn branches for each season of the year. Color the branches.

6. Turn the wheel to winter and add a triangle of white tissue paper to look like ice and snow.

7. Turn the wheel clockwise to spring and add colorful blossoms with marking pens.

8. Turn the wheel again. For summer, add leaves cut from the green construction paper scraps.

9. Glue the finished art to the black construction paper frame.

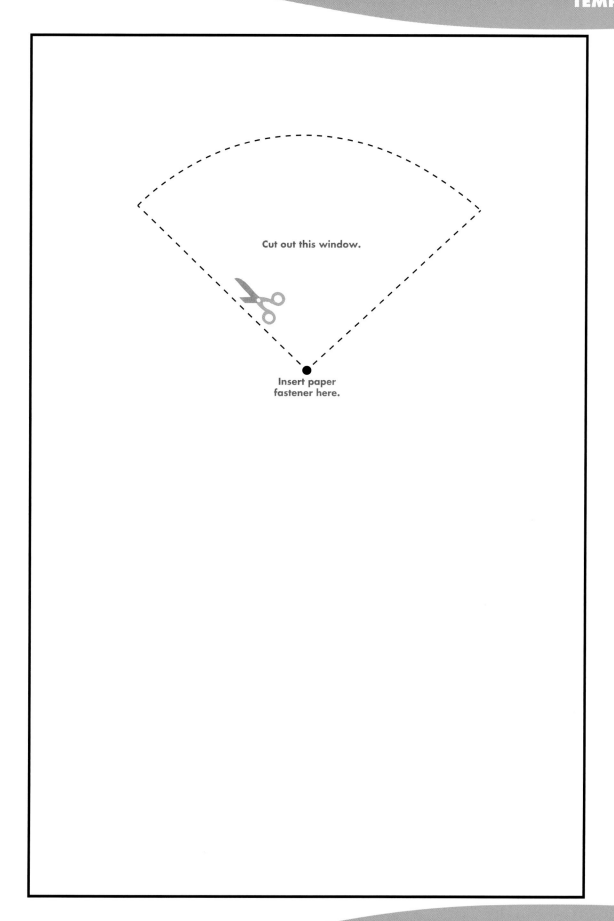

Cut out this window.

Insert paper
fastener here.

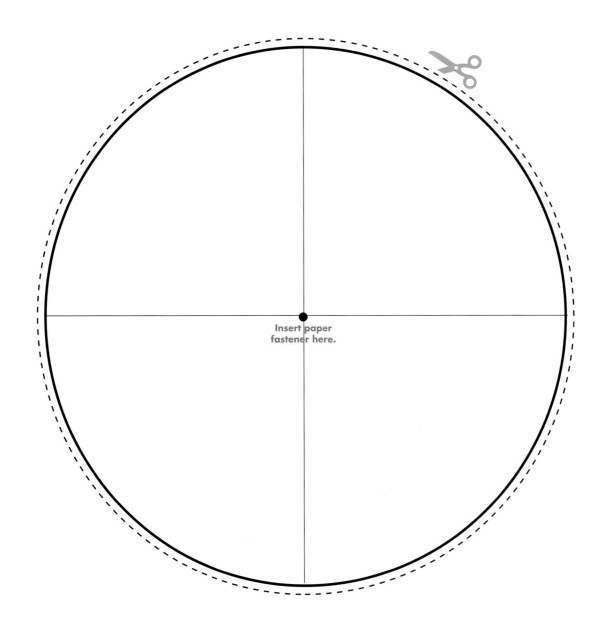

Insert paper
fastener here.

Jack-o'-lanterns have so many different expressions. Line up all your students' pumpkin chains on a bookcase or windowsill and watch them "watching you."

MATERIALS

- templates on the following page
- 4" x 18" (10 x 45.5 cm) orange construction paper
- 4" x 9" (10 x 23 cm) yellow construction paper
- green construction paper scraps
- black beans
- crayons, marking pens, or colored pencils
- scissors
- pencil
- tape
- glue
- hole punch

Jack-o'-Lantern Fun

STEPS TO FOLLOW

1. Fold the orange construction paper into quarters. Refold accordion style.

2. Trace lightly in pencil around the pumpkin template onto the folded orange paper.

3. Cut out the pumpkin shape.

4. Draw a smile line on each pumpkin. Use the hole punch to create "peek-through" pumpkin grins.

5. Cut eyes and noses for the pumpkins from the yellow construction paper.

6. Tape pieces of yellow paper behind the smiles.

7. Cut a stem and a vine from green construction paper scraps.

8. Curl the vine around the pencil.

9. Glue all cut pieces to the pumpkins.

10. Add black beans for eyes.

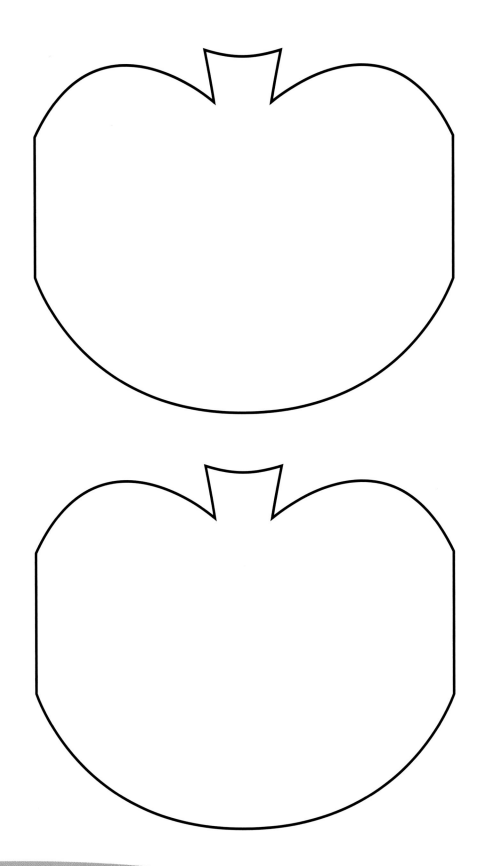

Fill your pumpkin patch with sponge-printed pumpkins enjoying a harvest moon.

MATERIALS

- 11" x 17" (28 x 43 cm) dark blue construction paper for the background
- 3" x 4" (7.5 x 10 cm) yellow construction paper for the moon
- 12" x 18" (30.5 x 45.5 cm) black construction paper for the frame
- 2" x 3" (5 x 7.5 cm) pieces of tissue paper in light pastel colors for the ghosts
- orange, black, and yellow tempera paint
- sponge cut into a pumpkin shape
- pencil with a new eraser
- silver or gold foil star stickers
- black fine-point marking pen
- shallow dishes

The Pumpkin Patch

STEPS TO FOLLOW

1. Draw a horizon line with the black marker.

2. Cut a moon shape from the yellow paper and glue it in place in the sky.

3. Pour puddles of paint into the dishes.

4. Dab the pumpkin sponge in the orange paint and print on the blue paper. Allow paint to dry.

5. Dip the pencil eraser in the yellow paint. Print yellow eyes and mouths on the pumpkins.

6. Use the black marker to outline the pumpkin shapes, add a curly vine, and make a black dot in each eye.

7. Round the top corners of the tissue paper pieces. Rip strips up from the bottom. Give the ghosts eyes, using the pencil eraser dipped in the black tempera paint.

8. Add foil stars in the sky.

Jack-o'-Lantern Pals

STEPS TO FOLLOW

1. Trace around the pumpkin template on the orange construction paper and cut out 4 pumpkins.

2. Cut the yellow strips as shown to create the pumpkin faces. Glue in place.

   nose   mouth   eyes

3. Glue on the black beans for eyes. Place the beans in a different position on each pumpkin.

4. Fold each pumpkin in half.

5. Glue the pumpkins back to back.

6. Slip the pipe cleaner between the stems and curl it.

Children will be delighted with their jack-o'-lantern pals, which can be taken home to use as table or window decorations.

MATERIALS

- templates on the following page
- 4—6" x 8" (15 x 20 cm) orange construction paper pieces for the pumpkins
- 4—1" x 6" (2.5 x 15 cm) yellow construction paper strips
- green pipe cleaner
- pencil
- black beans
- scissors
- glue

Pumpkin (orange)

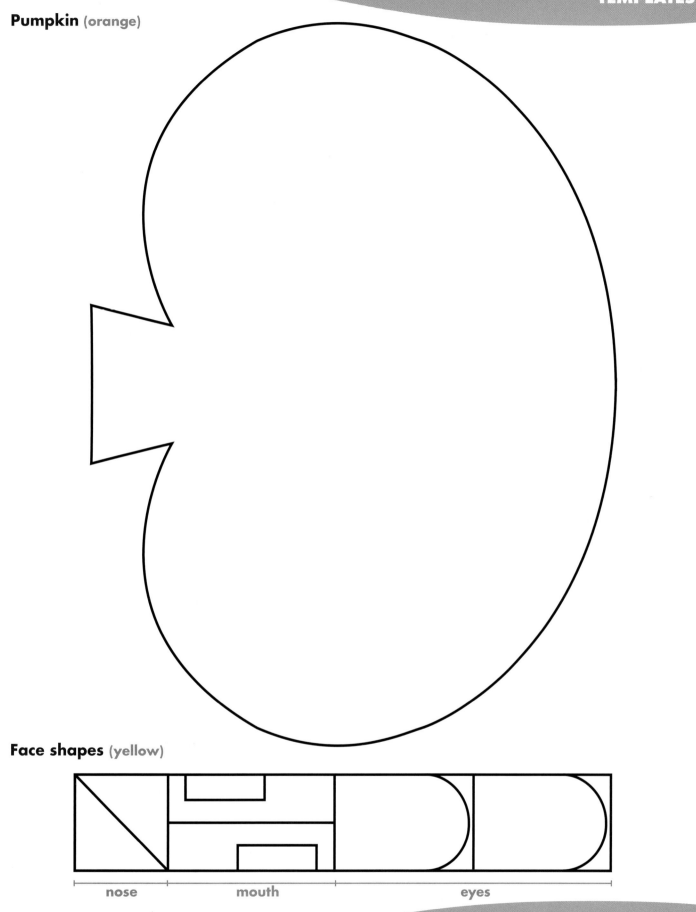

Face shapes (yellow)

nose   mouth   eyes

Positive–Negative Pumpkins

STEPS TO FOLLOW

1. Lay the orange paper on the right side of the black paper. Draw one-half of a pumpkin shape.

2. Cut out the shape and flip it over to the left side of the orange paper.

3. Draw one eye, half a nose, and half a mouth on the black paper. Flip it over onto the orange paper.

4. Glue the shapes in place.

Use orange and black construction paper to create striking jack-o'-lanterns. This project allows students to discover that when any shape is cut, there is a positive image and a negative image created at the same time. This activity is also effectively done with paper cut in smaller sizes.

MATERIALS

- 6" x 9" (15 x 23 cm) orange construction paper
- 9" x 12" (23 x 30.5 cm) black construction paper
- glue
- scissors
- pencil

This cat, made from basic shapes, has a 3-dimensional quality.

MATERIALS

- 9" x 12" (23 x 30.5 cm) dark blue construction paper for the background
- 4" (10 cm) square of yellow construction paper for the moon
- 9 ½ x 12 ½ (24 x 32 cm) yellow construction paper for the frame
- 3" x 7" (7.5 x 18 cm) black construction paper for the body and legs
- 2" x 4" (5 x 10 cm) black construction paper for the head and tail
- 2" x 12" (5 x 30.5 cm) brown construction paper for the fence
- scissors
- glue
- colored pencils
- hole punch

Black Cat on a Fence

STEPS TO FOLLOW

1. Fold the brown construction paper strip 3 times. Cut off one corner.

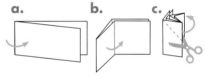

2. Glue the brown strip to the bottom of the blue sheet.

3. Cut out a large yellow circle for the moon. Glue it to the blue background.

4. Cut the black construction paper as shown for the cat's body parts. Use the hole punch and colored pencils to create the cat's face. Lay the pieces on the blue construction paper and arrange. Experiment with various poses and then glue in place.

The Changeable Cat

Students will have lots of fun drawing different facial expressions for their cats.

STEPS TO FOLLOW

1. Cut two 4½″ (11.5 cm) vertical slits in the white construction paper as shown.

2. Sketch the cat's head around the slits. Color in the whole area using the side of a broken black crayon.

3. Slip the white construction paper strip through the slits. Pull the strip all the way to one side. Sketch the face of the character on the first section of the strip.

4. Pull the strip to the next section. Draw the face again, showing a change of expression. Keep moving the strip and drawing until 4 different expressions are shown.

5. Add color to the pull strip.

6. Add details and color to the area around the outside of the cat's head. A colorful, repetitive border helps add interest.

7. Glue the top and the bottom of the white paper to the blue construction paper frame. Be sure the area in the middle is free of glue so the paper strip moves freely.

MATERIALS

- 9″ (23 cm) square of white construction paper

- 4″ x 18″ (10 x 45.5 cm) white construction paper strip

- 10″ (25.5 cm) square of blue construction paper for the frame

- crayons or marking pens

- scissors or craft knife

- ruler

Art for All Seasons • EMC 2001 • ©2004 by Evan-Moor Corp.

It's instant Halloween ambience when you have these 8-legged critters about the room.

MATERIALS

- 5" (12.5 cm) square of black construction paper for the body
- 3" x 6" (7.5 x 15 cm) black construction paper strip for the legs
- 2 ½" x 1" (6 x 2.5 cm) white construction paper for the eyes
- paper scraps in assorted colors
- paper clips
- glue
- scissors
- tape

Spider on a Line

STEPS TO FOLLOW

1. Fold the black square into quarters. Round off the outside corner.

2. Cut on one fold line into the center.

3. Roll and tape into a cone shape. As you create the cone, slip a string with a paper clip tied on the end inside.

4. Cut 8 spider legs from the black rectangle. Fold each one twice as shown.

5. Glue the first segment of each leg to the spider's body.

6. Cut the white paper for eyes. Add a black circle cut from scraps.

7. Add a mouth and other desired details with paper scraps in assorted colors.

8. Tie another paper clip onto the end of the string.

Body

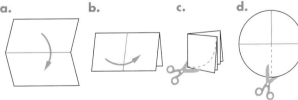

a.　　　b.　　　c.　　　d.

Legs

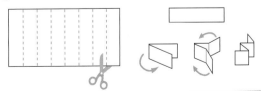

Furry Friends

STEPS TO FOLLOW

1. Trace around the bat template and cut out 3 bat shapes.

2. Punch 2 holes for each bat's eyes.

3. Add a mouth and other details with colored pencils.

4. Glue a small strip of colored paper behind the bats' eyes to make them look like they are glowing in the dark.

5. Create torn edges around the outside of the blue construction paper.

6. Fold down the tops of the bats' wings. Glue all the parts in place to create the finished product.

This project would make a great cover for student-created books about bats—real or imaginary.

MATERIALS

- templates on the following page
- 3—4" x 6" (10 x 15 cm) black construction paper pieces for the bats
- 12" (30.5 cm) square of dark blue construction paper for the background
- 12" (30.5 cm) square of yellow construction paper for the frame
- 2" (5 cm) square of yellow construction paper for the moon
- assorted colors of paper scraps
- hole punch
- scissors
- pencil
- colored pencils
- glue

Bats (black)

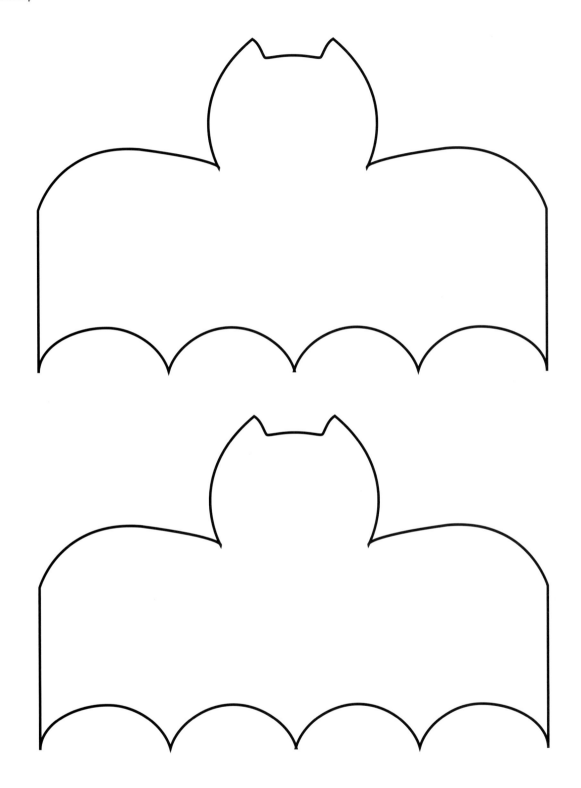

Silly Skeleton

This skeleton is sure to be a hit with students. They will enjoy making several versions, each in a different position.

MATERIALS

- patterns on the following page, reproduced for each student
- 8 ½" x 11" (21.5 x 28 cm) black construction paper for the background
- 9" x 12" (23 x 30.5 cm) orange construction paper for the frame
- hole punch
- scissors
- glue
- gel pens or crayons

STEPS TO FOLLOW

1. Cut out the pattern pieces.
2. Use the hole punch to make eye sockets.
3. Paste the various body parts to the black paper. Begin with the skull and spine. Add the ribs by putting glue on each end and letting the center of the strip buckle up. Bend the leg and arm strips at the joints before gluing down.
4. Glue the black paper to the orange frame.
5. Glue the poem to the backside and read it together.

Art for All Seasons • EMC 2001 • ©2004 by Evan-Moor Corp.

Glue this poem to the back of the skeleton.

My skeleton,
My bony, bony skeleton
Keeps me standing tall.
Without my bony skeleton,
All my parts would fall.

Bones

Head

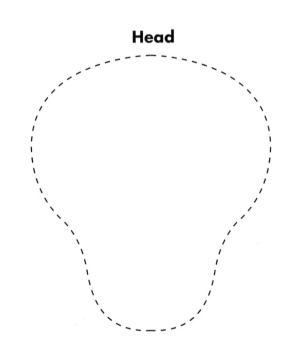

Ribs

Pelvis

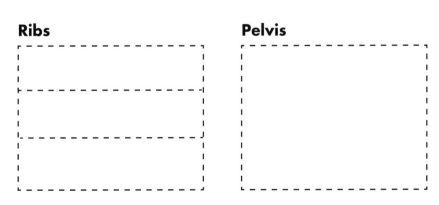

Follow up this project by having students write about who their creature is and what it does.

MATERIALS

- 8" x 11" (20 x 28 cm) white construction paper
- 6" (15 cm) square of yellow construction paper
- 9" x 12" (23 x 30.5 cm) black construction paper for the frame
- pumpkin seeds
- tempera paint and sponge pieces
- shallow dishes
- scissors
- glue
- fine-point marking pens
- pencil

Pumpkin Seed Smile

STEPS TO FOLLOW

1. Fold the yellow square of construction paper in half. Round the corners as shown.

2. Lay the folded circle on the white construction paper. Visualize a character. The folded part is its mouth. Sketch the outline of the character lightly in pencil.

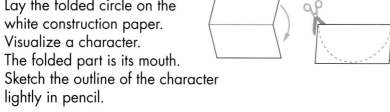

3. Sponge paint inside the shape. Let it dry thoroughly.

4. Glue the mouth in place.

5. Use the marking pens to add color and detail.

6. Glue the pumpkin seeds inside the character's mouth.

7. Add the black construction paper frame.

Turn this project into an entertaining display by posting clues as to the identity of each "ghost."

MATERIALS

- 2—7" x 10" (18 x 25.5 cm) white construction paper pieces for the ghost
- 8" x 11" (20 x 28 cm) blue construction paper for the background
- 9" x 12" (23 x 30.5 cm) yellow construction paper for the frame
- gold or silver foil star stickers
- crayons, marking pens, or colored pencils
- pencil
- scissors
- craft knife
- glue

Peek-a-Boo Ghost

STEPS TO FOLLOW

1. Lightly sketch a ghost on the white paper. Trace over that line with a black crayon or colored pencil. Cut just outside that line, holding the 2 sheets of white paper together. You now have 2 ghost shapes.

2. Glue one of the ghost shapes to the blue paper.

3. Glue the top edge of the second ghost shape to the first one.

4. After the glue has dried, lift up the top piece. Have students draw themselves inside the ghost costume. Let the feet extend below the white paper. Use crayons or colored pencils to add color to the drawing.

5. Add details to the front of the ghost shape: 2 eyes and a mouth.

6. Use the craft knife to cut out a moon shape from the blue construction paper.

7. Glue the blue paper to the yellow construction paper frame.

8. Add foil stars and other details with colored pencils.

A See-Through Ghost

Dangle these spooky creatures from your light fixtures to help celebrate the season.

MATERIALS

- newspaper
- 2—6" (15 cm) sheets of waxed paper, off the roll
- scraps of black construction paper
- scissors
- iron
- thread or clear plastic fishing line

STEPS TO FOLLOW

1. Place the 2 sheets of waxed paper together and cut out a ghost shape.

2. Cut eyes and a mouth from construction paper scraps. Lay them between the sheets of waxed paper.

3. Place the waxed paper between 2 sheets of newspaper. Press with a warm iron. (Adult supervision required.)

4. Fringe or rip the bottom of the ghost. This will make the ghost look as if it is floating through the air.

5. Punch a hole in the ghost and hang it with a piece of thread or plastic fishing line.

Extend this fanciful lesson by having students write about their Halloween goblins.

MATERIALS

- pattern on the following page, reproduced for each student
- 9" x 12" (23 x 30.5 cm) colored construction paper for the outside folder
- crayons, marking pens, or gel pens
- scissors
- glue
- pencil

"Trick or Treat" Goblin

STEPS TO FOLLOW

1. Follow the pop-up folding and cutting instructions as shown.

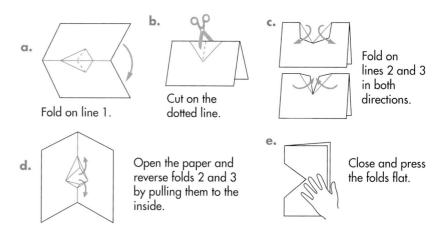

a. Fold on line 1.

b. Cut on the dotted line.

c. Fold on lines 2 and 3 in both directions.

d. Open the paper and reverse folds 2 and 3 by pulling them to the inside.

e. Close and press the folds flat.

2. Open the folded paper. Have the students sketch the goblin's body and facial features in pencil, using the pop-up portion as a mouth or a beak. They may then complete the picture by adding color.

3. Fold the construction paper in half.

4. Lay the folded pattern inside the folder. Draw a line in pencil inside the beak opening. Flip the pattern over and do the same on the other side. Use a white gel pen or a colored pencil to write "Trick or Treat" inside that area.

5. Apply glue to one side of the finished pop-up. Close the folder and press. Flip the folder over, open it, and apply glue to the other side of the pattern. Close the folder again and press firmly.

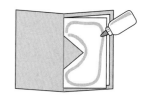

6. Add a title and decorations to the outside of the folder.

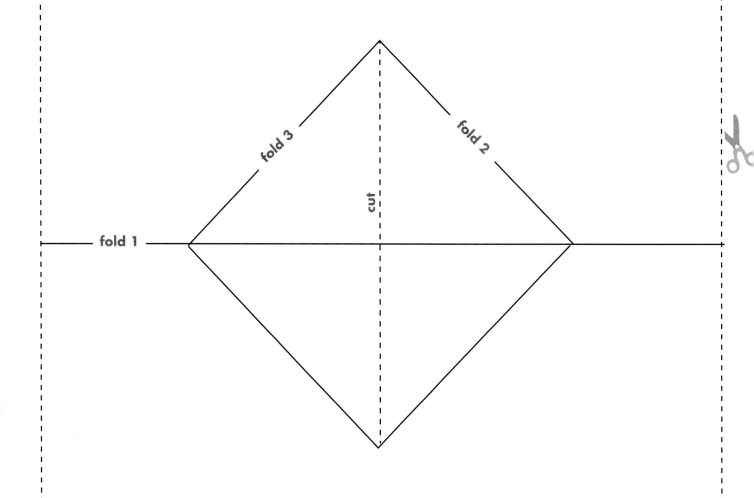

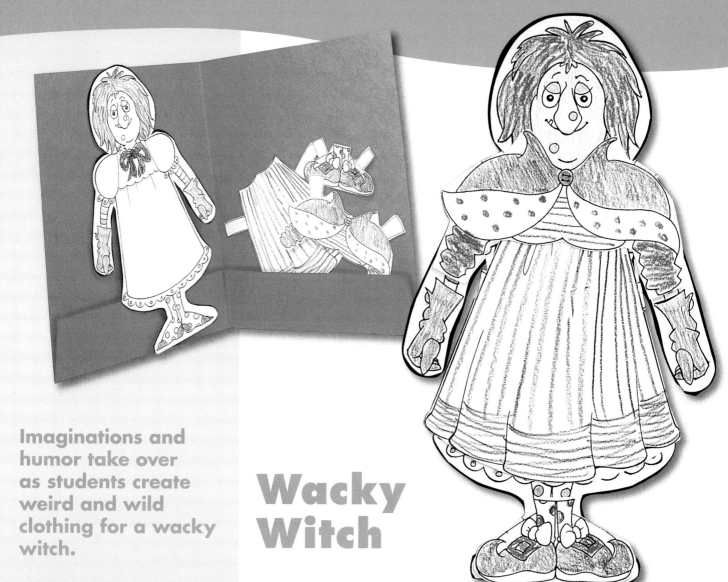

Imaginations and humor take over as students create weird and wild clothing for a wacky witch.

Wacky Witch

MATERIALS

- patterns on the following 2 pages, reproduced for each student
- 6" x 11" (15 x 28 cm) black construction paper for the backing behind the witch
- 12" x 16" (30.5 x 41 cm) orange construction paper for the folder
- crayons, marking pens, or colored pencils
- scissors
- stapler

STEPS TO FOLLOW

1. Color and cut out the paper doll pattern.

2. Glue Wacky Witch to the black construction paper. Trim around the outside.

3. Color the witch's wardrobe using the basic patterns provided.

4. Cut out the clothing items and try them on the paper doll.

5. Create a folder with a pocket to store Wacky Witch and her wardrobe. Fold the orange construction paper in half, and then fold up one edge. Staple the sides. Glue the label on the front.

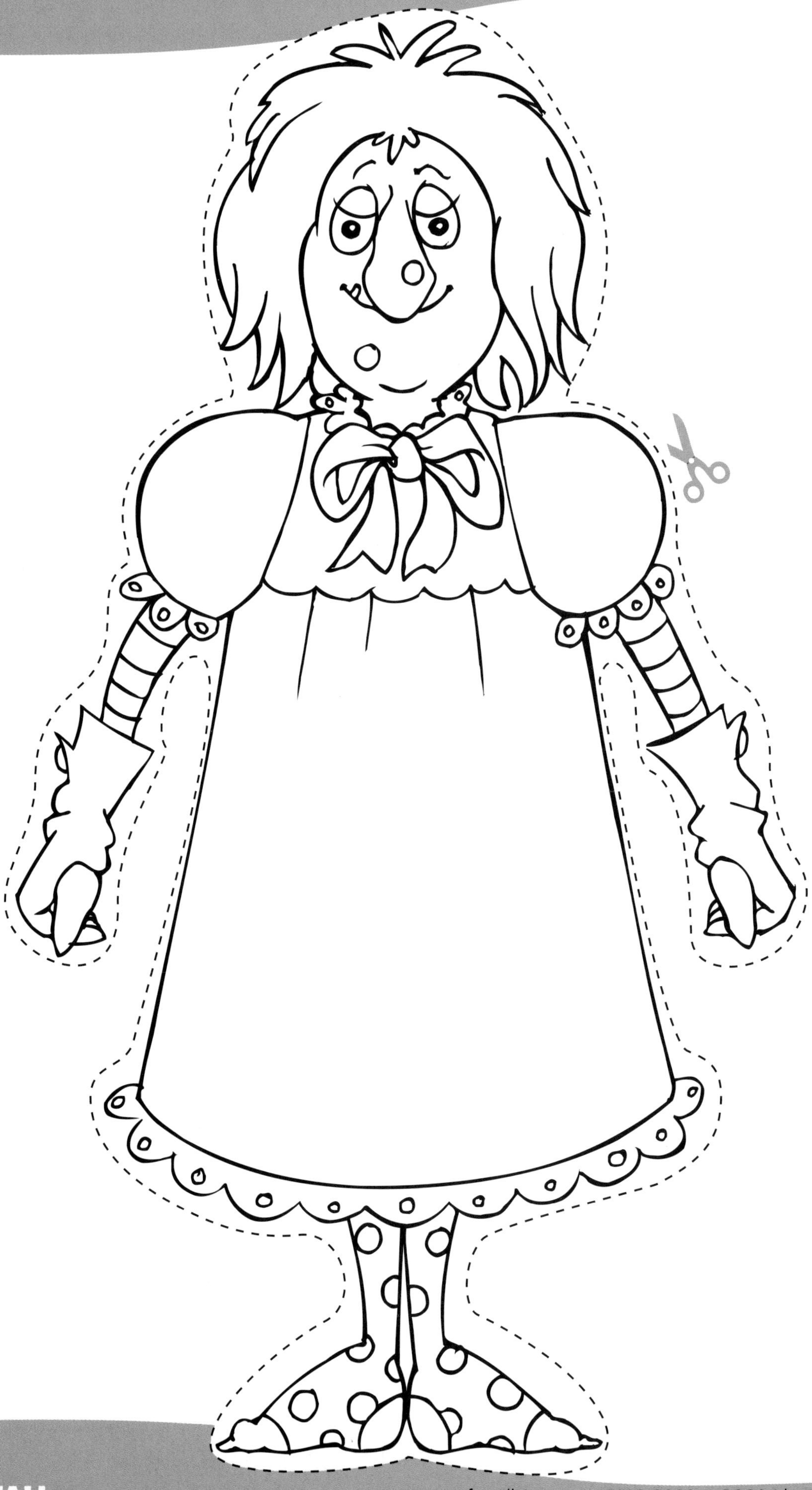

Wacky

Witch

The Dancing Witch

This little witch is perfect for hanging in the window to welcome Halloween. She wobbles and wiggles and has a message tucked under her cape.

MATERIALS

- templates and patterns on the following page
- 3" x 6" (7.5 x 15 cm) black construction paper for hats and boots
- 6" x 12" (15 x 30.5 cm) black construction paper for the basic witch
- 5" (12.5 cm) square of white or flesh-colored construction paper for the face and hands
- 2" x 6" (5 x 15 cm) orange construction paper for the hair and a jack-o'-lantern
- scissors
- glue
- paper fastener
- crayons, marking pens, or colored pencils
- hole punch
- yarn or cord
- wooden bead or paper clip

STEPS TO FOLLOW

1. Use the head template as a guide for cutting the head from the white construction paper. Add facial features with crayons or marking pens. Cut hair strips from the orange construction paper and glue them to the head.

2. Cut the cape from the black construction paper. Fold the cape as shown.

3. Cut the hat from the black construction paper using the template as a guide. Glue the hat to the head.

4. Cut boots using the template as a guide. Glue in place.

5. Attach the head to the cape using a paper fastener.

6. Cut the hands. Glue them on the cape.

7. Create a jack-o'-lantern from the orange construction paper scraps. Add details with crayons or marking pens. Glue the jack-o'-lantern in one hand of the witch.

8. Open the witch's cape and glue the Halloween greeting inside.

9. Punch a hole in the top of the hat and attach a length of cord and a bead for hanging.

Art for All Seasons • EMC 2001 • ©2004 by Evan-Moor Corp.

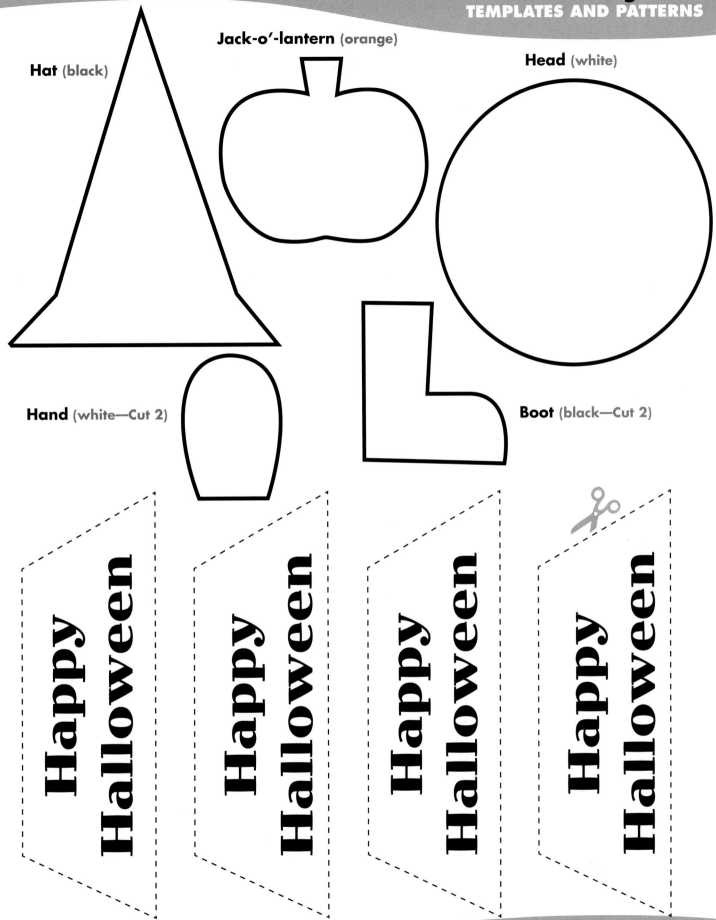

Hat (black)

Jack-o'-lantern (orange)

Head (white)

Hand (white—Cut 2)

Boot (black—Cut 2)

Happy Halloween

Happy Halloween

Happy Halloween

Happy Halloween

A Haunted House

After completing the project, brainstorm a list of vivid adjectives that might describe this haunted house and its inhabitants. Then write about it.

MATERIALS

- patterns on the following page, reproduced for each student
- 9" x 12" (23 x 30.5 cm) brown construction paper for the basic house
- 5" x 12" (12.5 x 30.5 cm) black construction paper for the roof
- 2" x 6" (5 x 15 cm) black construction paper for the shutters
- ruler
- scissors
- glue
- crayons, marking pens, or colored pencils

STEPS TO FOLLOW

1. Fold up the bottom 2" (5 cm) of the brown construction paper for the porch. Accordion-fold the bottom section as shown.

   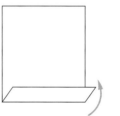

2. Color and cut out the patterns. Glue the windows and door to the house.

3. Cut the shutter pieces and fold back side flaps to create a hinged area to glue to the house.

   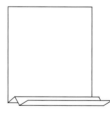

4. Rip a delapidated old roof from the black construction paper. Glue in place.

5. Glue the pumpkins on the front porch and the cat in the doorway.

6. Use the bubble pattern to show what sounds are coming from this haunted house.

7. Add the Home Sweet Home sign.

Art for All Seasons • EMC 2001 • ©2004 by Evan-Moor Corp.

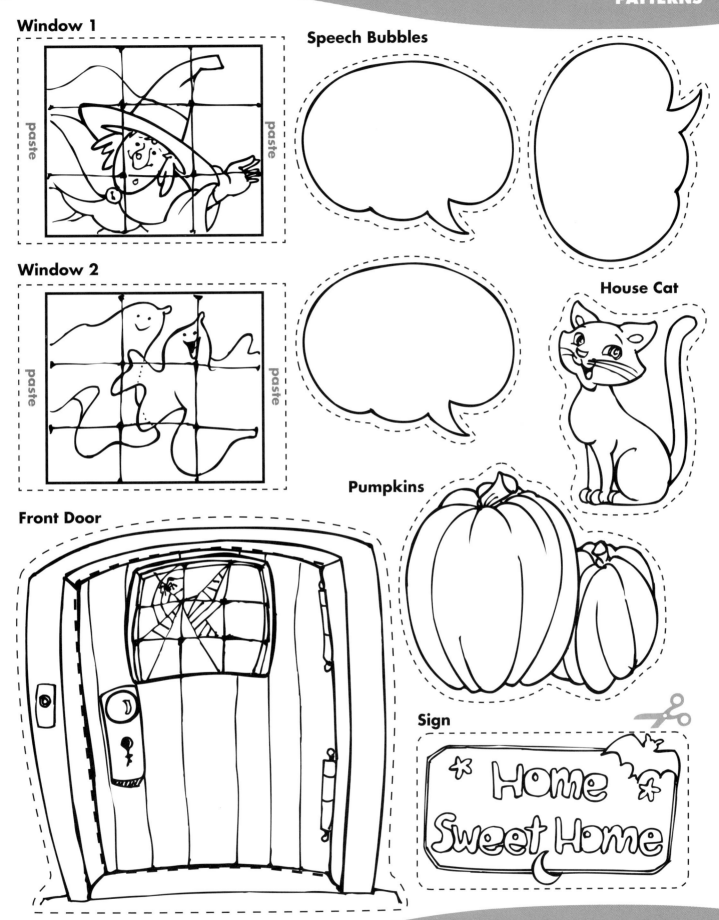

Window 1

Speech Bubbles

paste   paste

Window 2

House Cat

paste   paste

Pumpkins

Front Door

Sign

Home Sweet Home

Columbus Sails

STEPS TO FOLLOW

1. Fold down approximately 1" (2.5 cm) of the blue paper. Flip the paper over and continue to accordion-fold the paper. Set the paper on the table to create the impression of a rough blue sea.

2. Cut the front edge of the folded paper in a wave pattern.

3. Color and cut out the 3 ship patterns and sails.

4. Glue the ships to the brown construction paper. Trim around the edges.

5. Attach the pipe cleaners to the ships using a strip of tape across the back.

6. Punch the holes in the sails as marked.

7. Slip the sails over the pipe cleaners as shown.

8. Use tape to attach the flags to the tops of the pipe cleaners.

9. Glue the ships onto the "waves" in the blue paper.

Before doing this project, share books that tell about Columbus's journey. After completing the project, have students write about the adventures and disappointments of the voyage.

MATERIALS

- patterns on the following page, reproduced for each student

- 12" (30.5 cm) square of blue construction paper

- 4" x 8" (10 x 20 cm) brown construction paper for the backing of the ships

- 3 strips of pipe cleaner for the masts—2" (5 cm), 3" (7.5 cm), and 4" (10 cm)

- hole punch

- scissors

- crayons, marking pens, or colored pencils

- tape

- glue

Flags

Niña

Pinta

Santa María

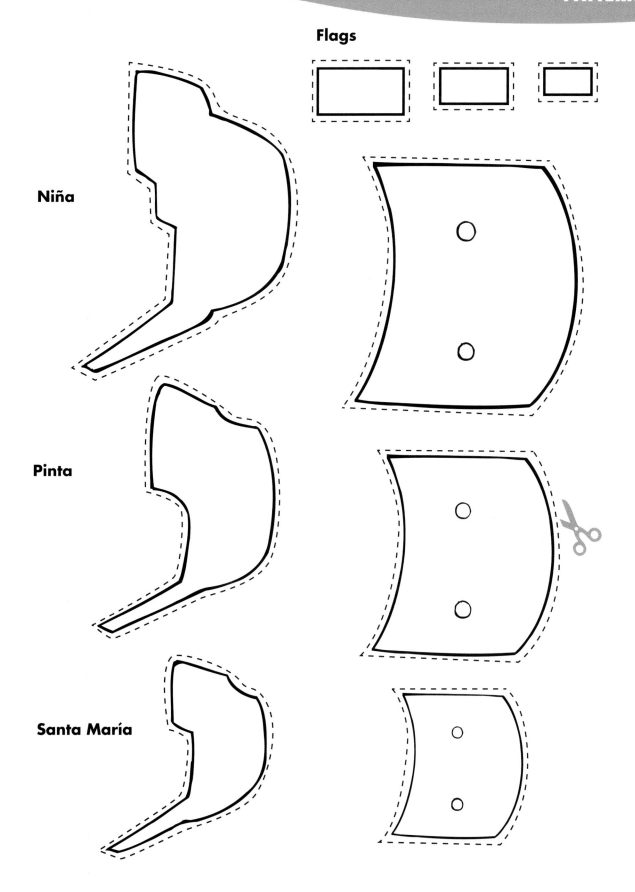

The Harvest Cornucopia

Discuss the meaning of a cornucopia as a "horn of plenty." How was that symbol important in colonial America? What meaning does it have today?

STEPS TO FOLLOW

1. Color and cut out the pattern for the mouth of the basket.

2. Glue the pattern to the black paper.

3. Cut the slit as marked using a craft knife. Cut through both the pattern and the black construction paper.

4. Draw a pencil line to outline the basket shape. Build the basket by tearing off bits of brown construction paper and gluing them around the mouth of the basket. Begin gluing at the top of the basket and overlap the pieces as you work down.

5. Slip the white construction paper strip into the slit in the mouth of the basket. On the strip, draw or create with cut paper all the fruits and vegetables we enjoy in the fall. Slip the strip back into the cornucopia. Then pull the strip out again to show the abundance of the harvest.

6. Use a strip of double-stick tape along the top of the black paper to attach it to the yellow paper frame.

MATERIALS

- pattern and template on the following 2 pages

- 9" x 12" (23 x 30.5 cm) white construction paper to use in cutting out the template

- 9" x 12" (23 x 30.5 cm) black construction paper for the background

- 6" x 12" (15 x 30.5 cm) brown construction paper for the basket

- 9 ½" x 12 ½" (24 x 32 cm) yellow construction paper for the frame

- craft knife

- scissors

- glue

- double-stick tape

- crayons, marking pens, or colored pencils

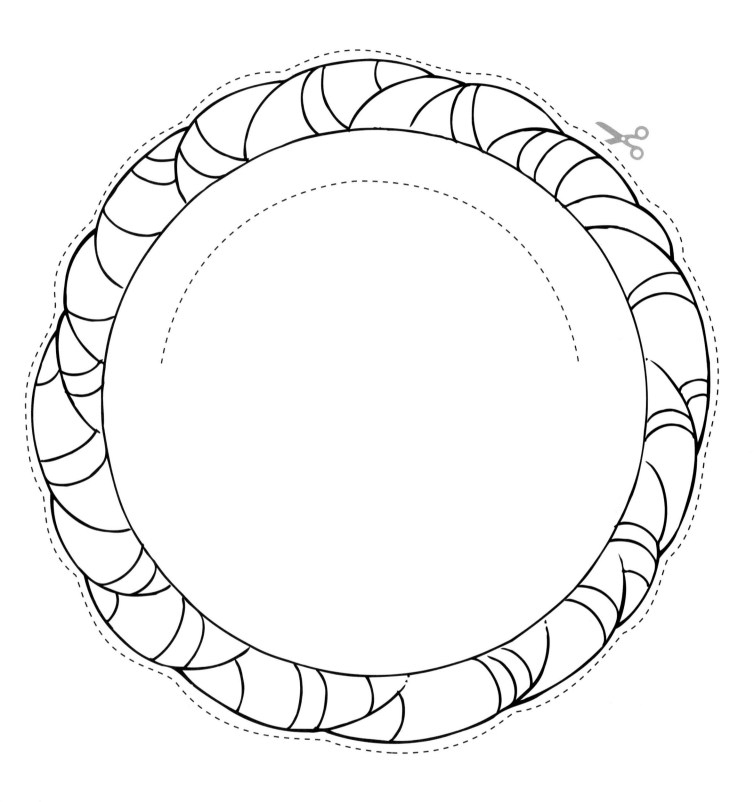

Cornucopia Pull-out (white)

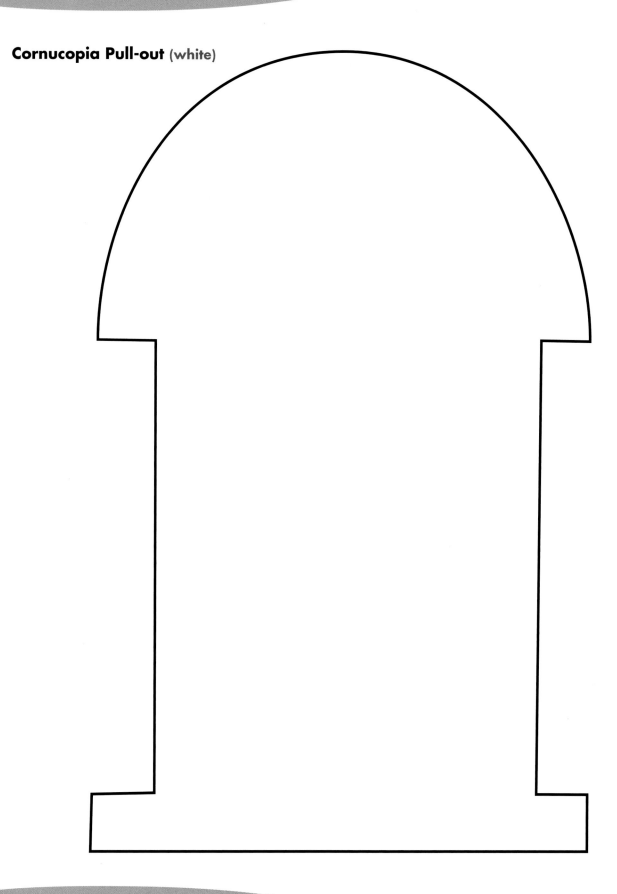

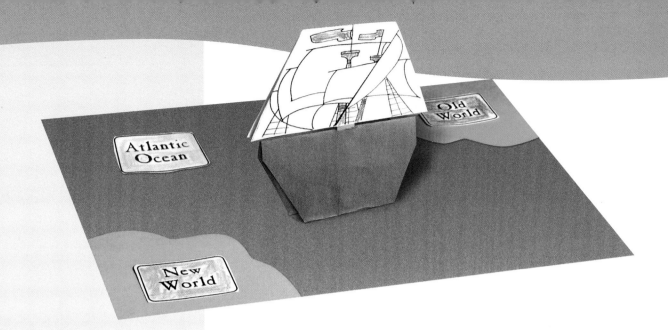

Create a scene that helps tell the story of the Pilgrims crossing the Atlantic in their little ship.

MATERIALS

- patterns on the following page, reproduced for each student
- 9" x 12" (23 x 30.5 cm) blue construction paper for the ocean
- 3 ½" x 5" (9 x 12.5 cm) brown construction paper for the ship
- 2—4" (10 cm) squares of green construction paper
- scissors
- glue and double-stick tape
- craft stick
- crayons, marking pens, or colored pencils

The Mayflower

STEPS TO FOLLOW

1. Fold the brown construction paper in half, and then fold the ends in ¾" (2 cm). Trim the corners as shown.

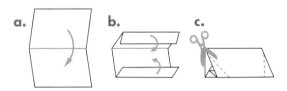

2. Fold out a flap on the bottom of the ship.

3. Color, fold, and cut out the sail pattern.

4. Place a strip of double-stick tape on each side of the top half of the craft stick. Place the taped area of the stick inside the sails and press flat.

5. Make a small slit in the top folded edge of the ship. Slip the craft stick through the slit and tape it to the inside of the ship. Set the ship on the blue paper and arrange it so that it is sailing toward the west.

6. Cut the green squares as shown. Glue these in opposite corners of the blue paper. Add the labels Old World and New World cut from the pattern page. Discuss with students how maps are oriented with west to the left and east to the right. Remind them that the New World was to the west, so this label needs to be on the left-hand side. Add the label for the Atlantic Ocean.

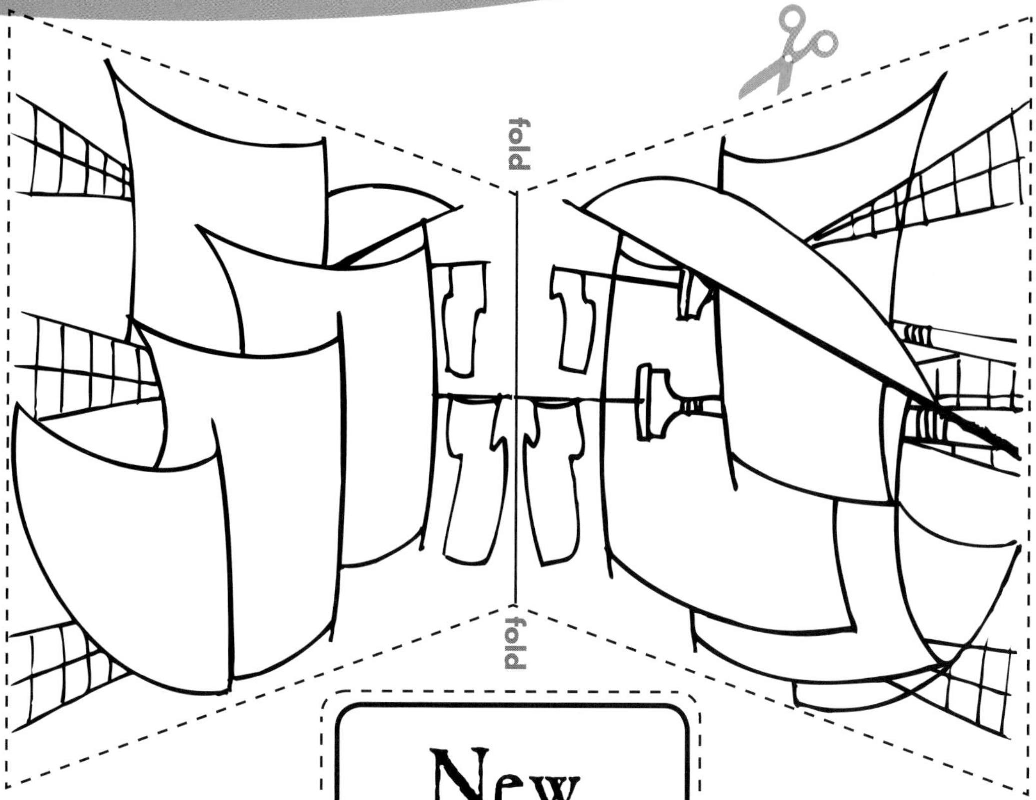

fold

fold

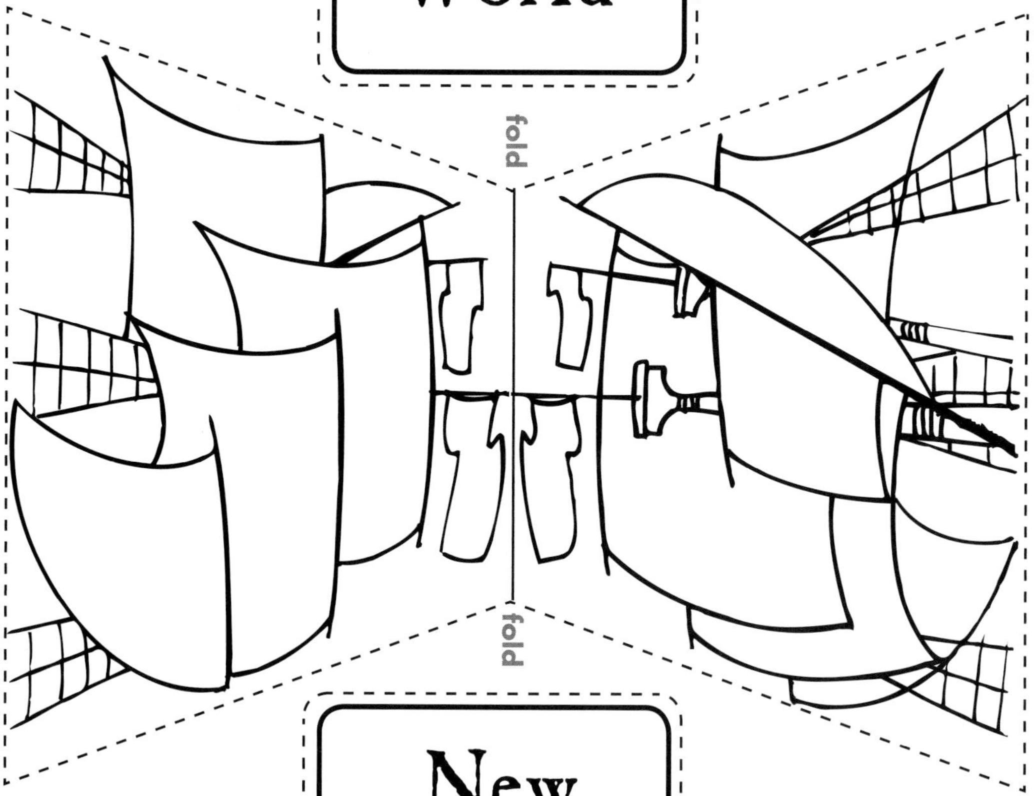

fold

fold

Atlantic Ocean

Old World

New World

Atlantic Ocean

Old World

New World

Students create a Pilgrim boy to sit on their desks. They can write all the things they are thankful for on the ears of corn and slip them into the Pilgrim's built-in pocket.

A Cross-Legged Pilgrim

MATERIALS

- patterns on the following page, reproduced for each student
- 7" (18 cm) square of black construction paper for the body
- scissors
- glue
- crayons, marking pens, or colored pencils
- stapler

STEPS TO FOLLOW

1. Fold the basic cross-legged body as shown. Trim off the tips of the feet and the top.

a.

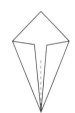

Fold into middle.

b.

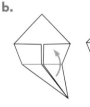

Fold up.

c.

Cut up to the fold.

d.

Cross over the legs and staple. Staple the pocket. Trim off points.

2. Color and cut out the patterns and glue them to the basic body shape.

3. Cut out the corn. List one thing on each ear that you are thankful for. Slip the corn into the Pilgrim's pocket.

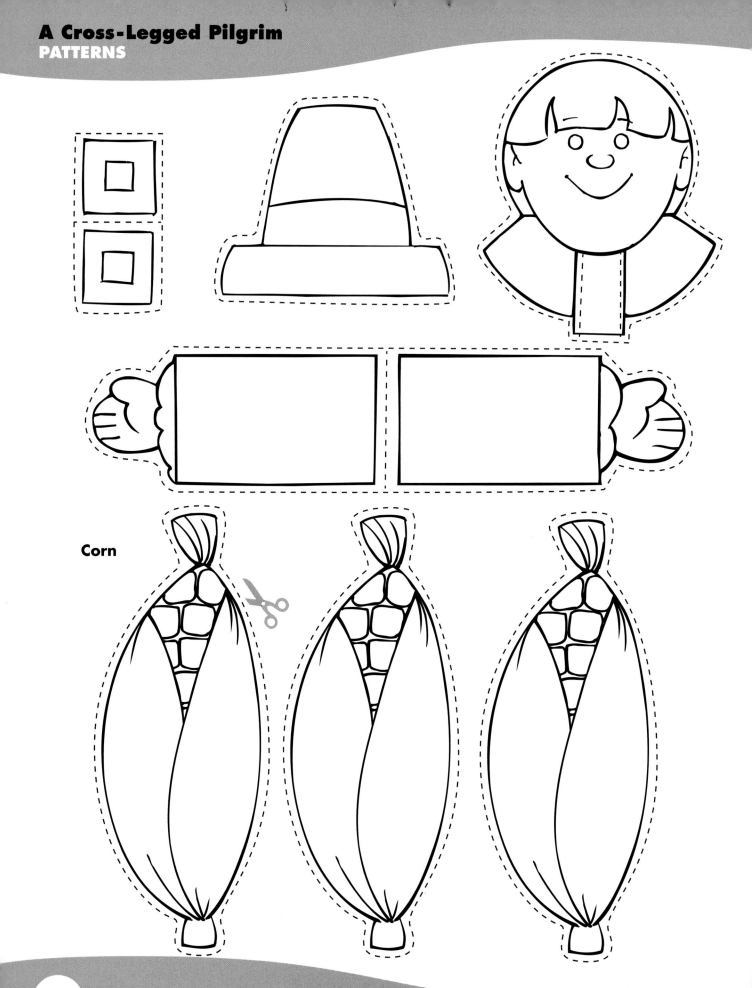

Corn

Students will be fascinated to learn about the layers of clothing that a typical Pilgrim girl wore each day. This activity gives them the opportunity to learn the names and functions of the various clothing items and compare them with what we wear today.

MATERIALS

- patterns on the following 2 pages, reproduced for each student
- 12" (30.5 cm) square of blue construction paper for the background
- 8" x 9" (20 x 23 cm) brown construction paper for the cape
- scissors
- glue or double-stick tape
- crayons, marking pens, or colored pencils

Little Miss Pilgrim

STEPS TO FOLLOW

1. Share books from the library on this topic with your students. Show them examples of the styles and colors worn by the Pilgrims. Stress that they wore a variety of darker, subdued colors in addition to black and gray.

2. Color and cut out the patterns.

3. Begin dressing Little Miss Pilgrim:

    a. Glue her stockings, garters, and shoes under her underdress.
    b. Glue her first petticoat over her underdress at the waistline.
    c. Glue the second petticoat over the first.
    d. Now glue her apron on top.
    e. Glue the pocket hanging from her apron.
    f. Glue or tape the top of the waistcoat at the neckline.
    g. Glue her doll in her hand.

4. Trim the brown cape paper as shown. Fold down the collar flaps. Glue the cape to the blue paper.

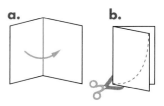

5. Glue Little Miss Pilgrim into the cape.

6. Add details with crayons, marking pens, or colored pencils.

Little Miss Pilgrim
PATTERNS

Pocket: Glue to the apron.

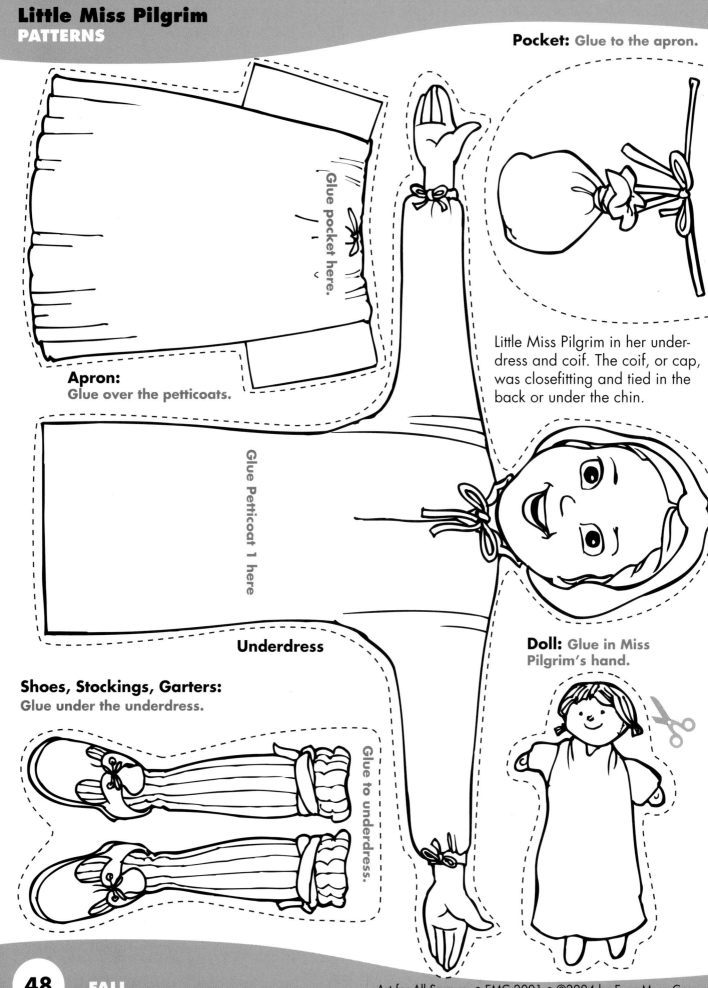

Glue pocket here.

Apron:
Glue over the petticoats.

Little Miss Pilgrim in her underdress and coif. The coif, or cap, was closefitting and tied in the back or under the chin.

Glue Petticoat 1 here

Underdress

Doll: Glue in Miss Pilgrim's hand.

Shoes, Stockings, Garters:
Glue under the underdress.

Glue to underdress.

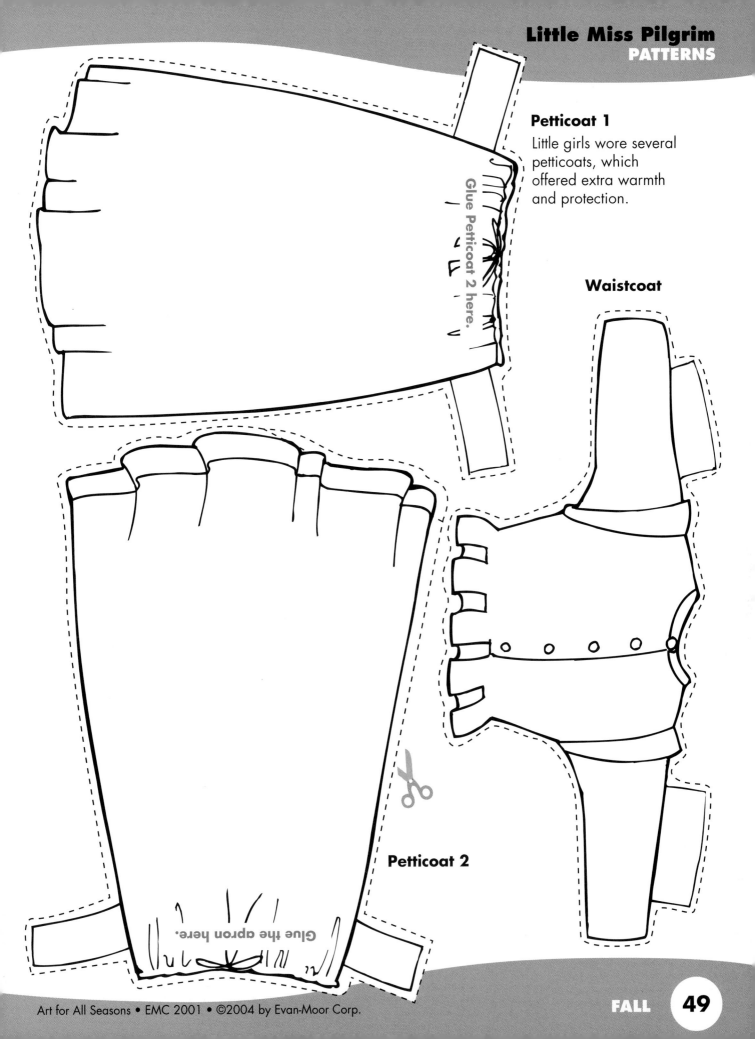

Petticoat 1

Little girls wore several petticoats, which offered extra warmth and protection.

Waistcoat

Glue Petticoat 2 here.

Petticoat 2

Glue the apron here.

A Native American

This Native American played a very important part in the Thanksgiving harvest feast. This 3-D representation has movable parts and can sit on your arm or the edge of a student's desk. He can be a rich addition to a Thanksgiving unit of study.

MATERIALS

- patterns on the following page, reproduced for each student
- 6" x 12" (15 x 30.5 cm) brown construction paper for the body
- 2—2" x 5" (5 x 12.5 cm) brown construction paper strips for the arms
- 5" (12.5 cm) square of black construction paper for the head
- ½" x 3" (1.25 x 7.5 cm) black construction paper strips for the braids
- 1" x 5" (2.5 x 12.5 cm) yellow construction paper for the headband
- 2 feathers
- 2 paper fasteners
- 3 colorful beads
- 10" (25.5 cm) strip of brown yarn

STEPS TO FOLLOW

1. Color and cut out the pattern pieces for the face and hands.

2. Fold the brown piece of construction paper for the body as shown.

3. Cut the legs up to the center line and round off the toes.

4. Round the top 2 corners on the brown strips for the arms. Glue one hand to the end of each arm.

5. Glue the face to the head as shown. Round off the top corners.

6. Glue the yellow headband in place and trim to fit. Slip the feathers under the headband and secure.

7. Glue the head to the body. Slip the beads onto the yarn and tie it around the neck.

8. Use paper fasteners to attach the arms.

9. Cut black strips to roll, glue, and make into a paper-chain effect for braids.

10. Add other details with crayons or marking pens.

a.   b.   c.

Step 4

Art for All Seasons • EMC 2001 • ©2004 by Evan-Moor Corp.

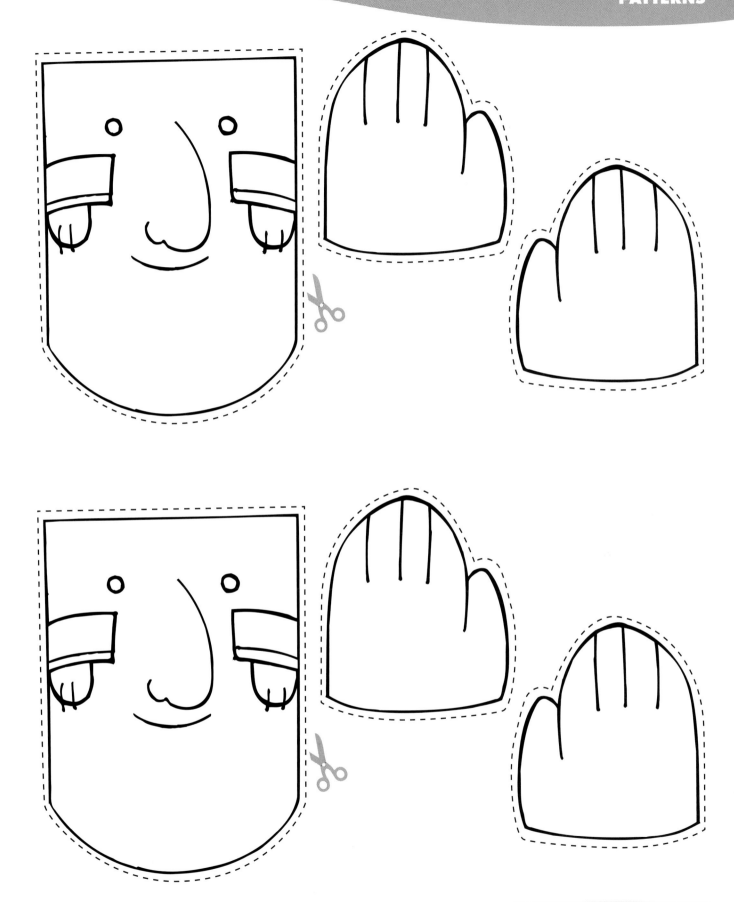

An Outstanding Turkey

STEPS TO FOLLOW

1. Use a pencil to trace the circle template onto the blue paper approximately 2" (5 cm) from the bottom edge.

2. Curl one end of each of the tail feathers around the pencil.

3. Alternate colors and glue the feathers in an arch around the top of the template line.

4. Cut the brown construction paper as shown. Round the corners for the body and wing pieces.

5. Cut the head from the red paper and add details with a marking pen and/or paper scraps.

6. Fold the brown paper spacers twice. Refold in accordion fashion. Glue them to the back of the turkey body. Then glue it all in place over the feathers.

7. Fold down a flap on each wing. Place glue on the bottom of the flap, slip it under the body piece, and hold in place until it is dry.

8. Cut twigs to size for the legs and feet. Glue in place.

This turkey gobbler has a colorful fanned tail and a spacer that holds the body and head away from the background paper to give it a 3-D quality.

MATERIALS

- 4" (10 cm) circle template cut from tagboard

- 11 ½" (29 cm) square of blue construction paper for the background

- 12" (30.5 cm) square of yellow construction paper for the frame

- 5" x 9" (12.5 x 23 cm) brown construction paper for the body and wings

- 2" x 3" (5 x 7.5 cm) red construction paper for the head

- 2—1" x 3" (2.5 x 7.5 cm) brown construction paper strips for the spacers

- 1" x 6" (2.5 x 15 cm) strips of assorted colors of construction paper for the feathers

- twigs

- scissors

- pencil

- glue

- crayons, marking pens, or colored pencils

Contents

A Chain of Ice Skaters

This project will brighten your windowsill or the top of your library center bookcase. Students will enjoy placing their chains end to end and creating a long line of happy skaters winding around your classroom.

STEPS TO FOLLOW

1. Accordion-fold the white paper as shown.

a.
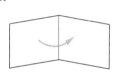

b.

c.

2. Lay the chain template on the folded paper. Trace around it in pencil and cut on the pencil line.

3. Open the chain. Use the hat templates to create a colorful winter hat for each skater. Glue them in place. Save the scraps to reuse as scarves and mittens if desired.

4. Use the crayons, marking pens, or colored pencils to create the rest of the skaters' clothing.

5. Cut the blue construction paper in a free-form shape to create the effect of a skating rink.

MATERIALS

- templates on the following page
- 7" x 18" (18 x 45.5 cm) white construction paper for the paper chain
- 1 ½" x 3" (4 x 7.5 cm) pieces of red, yellow, blue, and orange construction paper for the hats
- 9" x 12" (23 x 30.5 cm) light blue construction paper for the rink
- crayons, marking pens, or colored pencils
- pencil
- scissors
- glue

Hats (red, yellow, blue, orange)

Paper Chain Ice Skaters (white)

Hibernating Bear

Here's a fun way to sum up a unit on hibernation. Students will enjoy pulling down the flap to expose the sleeping bear.

MATERIALS

- patterns on the following page, reproduced for each student
- 9" x 12" (23 x 30.5 cm) blue construction paper for the background
- 5" x 9" (12.5 x 23 cm) brown construction paper for the hill
- 3" x 4" (7.5 x 10 cm) black construction paper for the cave opening
- 2" (5 cm) square of yellow construction paper for the moon
- 1" x 6" (2.5 x 15 cm) green construction paper for the trees
- glue
- crayons, marking pens, or colored pencils
- scissors

STEPS TO FOLLOW

a. Fold in half.

b. Fold the back piece down.

1. Fold the blue paper.

2. Tear a hill shape from the brown construction paper. Lay it on the top half of the blue paper. Cut a cave opening from the black paper. Lay it on the brown paper. Tear little pine trees from the green paper and glue them over the hillside. Cut a moon from the yellow paper and place it in the night sky.

3. Adjust all of the pieces and glue them in place.

4. Add details with a black colored pencil or marking pen.

5. Color and cut out the patterns. Students write a definition of *hibernation* in the box provided. Glue the patterns on the bottom half of the blue paper.

6. Fold the pattern and blue paper on the fold line.

fold

Hibernation is

_____

_____

_____

Cross-Legged Snowman

This cross-legged character has a built-in pocket for holding practice cards, story starters, or unexpected surprises.

STEPS TO FOLLOW

1. Fold the basic cross-legged body as shown.

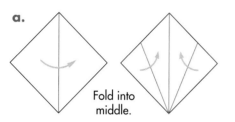

a.

Fold into middle.

b.

Fold up.

c.

Cut up to the fold.

d.

Cross over the legs and staple. Staple the pocket. Trim off points.

2. Use the template to cut several snowballs from the white construction paper. Use one of these for the snowman's head.

3. Cut a red hat, using the template as a guide. Cut the slit as shown with a craft knife and slip it over the top of the snowman's head. Glue in place.

4. Add the black beans for eyes and other details to the head and hat with cut paper and/or marking pens or colored pencils.

5. Glue the head to the top of the body.

6. Round off the tips of the snowman's feet.

7. Punch 2 holes on each side of the body. Insert the twigs for arms.

MATERIALS

- templates on the following page
- 9" (23 cm) square of white construction paper for basic cross-legged body
- several 3" (7.5 cm) squares of white construction paper for the head and snowballs
- 2" x 4" (5 x 10 cm) red construction paper for the hat
- 2" (5 cm) squares of yellow and blue construction paper for adding details
- 2 black beans
- 2 twigs
- hole punch
- craft knife
- scissors
- glue
- crayons, marking pens, or colored pencils
- stapler

Art for All Seasons • EMC 2001 • ©2004 by Evan-Moor Corp.

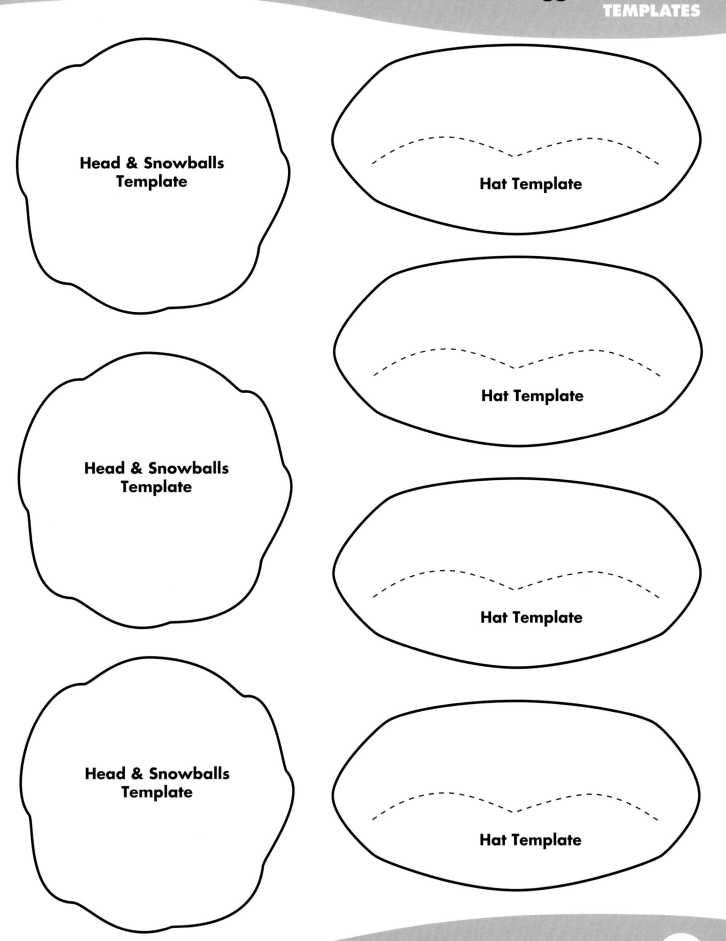

Head & Snowballs
Template

Hat Template

Head & Snowballs
Template

Hat Template

Hat Template

Head & Snowballs
Template

Hat Template

Penguin Playground

This whimsical project will motivate students to write stories or reports on penguins.

STEPS TO FOLLOW

1. Trim the ends of the white strip as shown. Apply a spot of glue to each end. Set the white paper on the blue paper, leaving a hump in the middle. Hold down the glued ends until dry.

2. Round off the top corners of the 3 penguin bodies. Fold up a ¼" (0.6 cm) flap on the bottom of each one.

3. Cut each of the black wing strips in half. Round off 2 of the corners on each. Experiment with different ways to place the wings on the bodies.

4. Add the eyes and beak with crayons, marking pens, or colored pencils. Now glue the wings in place.

5. Apply glue to the flap on the bottom of each penguin. Place them on the white ice flow, holding them in place until the glue is dry enough to hold.

MATERIALS

- 3" x 12" (7.5 x 30.5 cm) white construction paper strip for the ice floe

- 5" x 12" (12.5 x 30.5 cm) blue construction paper for the sea

- 3—2" x 3 ½" (5 x 9 cm) white construction paper pieces for the penguins' bodies

- 3—1" x 3" (2.5 x 7.5 cm) black construction paper strips for the penguins' wings

- crayons, marking pens, or colored pencils

- glue

- scissors

This activity teaches students that every shape has a positive and a negative aspect. Students will enjoy experimenting with different patterns and colors.

MATERIALS

- templates on the following page
- 6" x 9" (15 x 23 cm) colored construction paper for the background
- 3" x 9" (7.5 x 23 cm) white construction paper
- 7" x 10" (18 x 25.5 cm) black construction paper for the frame
- scissors
- glue
- pencil

Positive-Negative Trees

STEPS TO FOLLOW

1. Lay a template on the lower edge of the white paper. Trace around the template. Cut on those lines. Keep the cutout shapes in a pile.

2. Glue what is left of the white paper to the top edge of the colored paper.

3. Lay the cutout pieces back into their original place in the white paper. Apply glue to each shape and then flip them over and place them so the bottom edges are touching. Continue until all the shapes have been turned over.

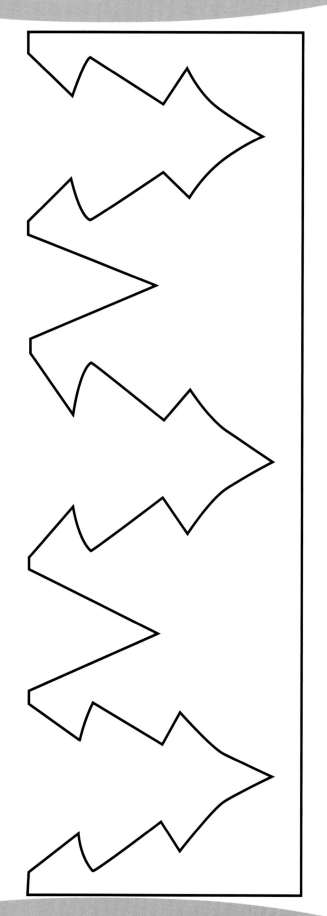

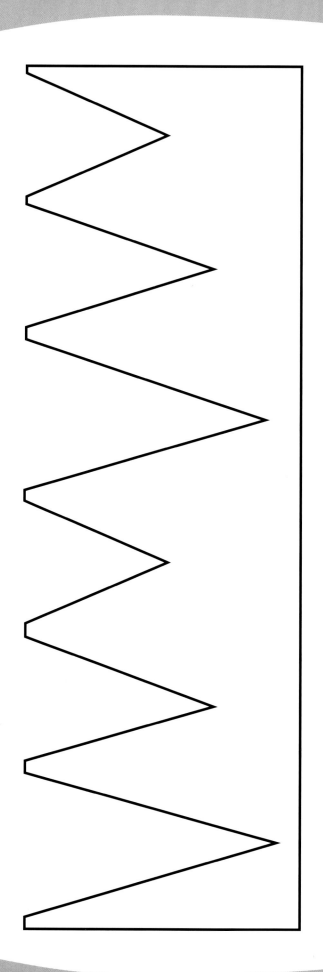

These toboggan kids make a spectacular winter bulletin board. Place them on a white hill and add the caption "Winter Wonderland."

MATERIALS

- patterns on the following page, reproduced for each student
- 4" x 9" (10 x 23 cm) red construction paper for the sled
- 7 ½" x 6 ½" (19 x 16.5 cm) white construction paper for the backing of the kids
- crayons, marking pens, or colored pencils
- pencil
- scissors
- glue
- hole punch
- 10" (25.5 cm) of roving or yarn

Toboggan Kids

STEPS TO FOLLOW

1. Roll one end of the red paper around a pencil to create the front of the toboggan.

2. Color all the patterns.

3. Glue the kid patterns to the white construction paper, and then cut them out.

4. Glue on the hats and scarves.

5. Fold the patterns on the fold line. Apply glue to the flaps and place them on the toboggan. Hold in place until the glue dries.

6. Punch a hole on each side of the rolled front of the toboggan. Insert the roving on each side and tie in a knot. Glue the roving in the hands of the first kid.

Kids

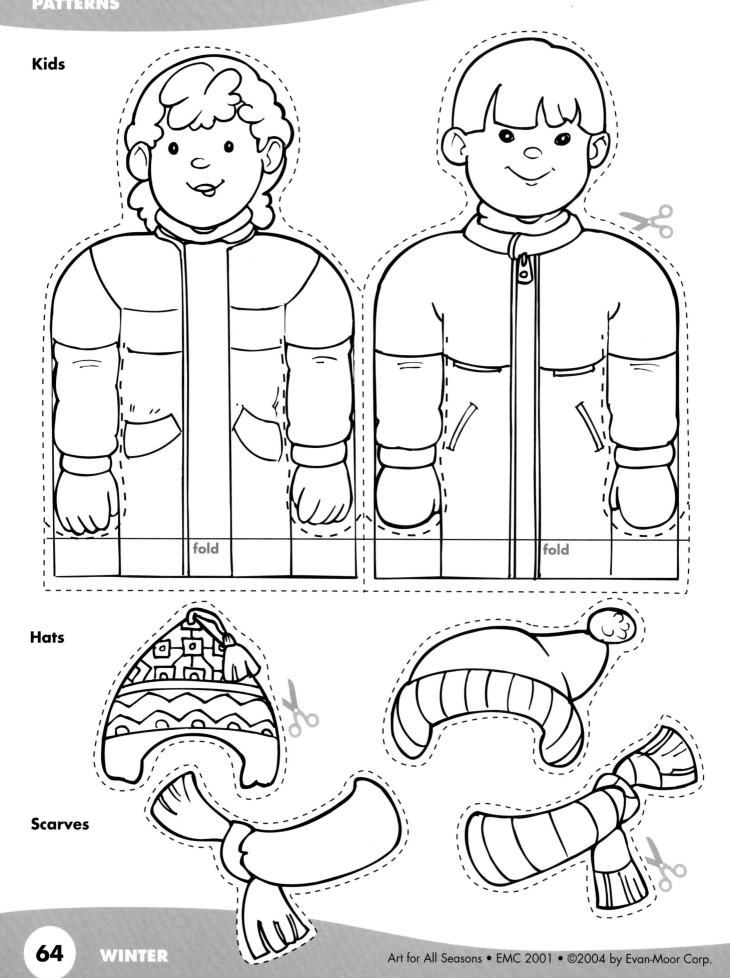

fold

fold

Hats

Scarves

Send a pop-up card to celebrate the "Festival of Lights."

MATERIALS

- patterns on the following page, reproduced for each student
- 5 ½" x 9" (14 x 23 cm) blue construction paper for the outside folder
- 1" x 2" (2.5 x 5 cm) red construction paper for the candle
- 1" x 1 ½" (2.5 x 4 cm) yellow construction paper for the flame
- hole punch
- yellow roving
- scissors
- glue

Happy Hanukkah

Hanukkah Pop-Up Card

Celebrating Hanukkah,
Add one candle every night.
The menorah spreads a special light.

STEPS TO FOLLOW

1. Follow the cutting and folding directions on the patterns.

Pop-up A		Pop-up B	
a.	b.	a.	b.
c.	d.	c.	d.

2. Add color and designs to Pop-up B.

3. Fold the blue outside folder in half. Lay Pop-up A into the fold. Apply glue to the exposed side of the pop-up. Close the folder and press firmly. Flip the folder over. Open and apply glue to the other side of the pop-up. Close the folder and press. Allow to dry. Follow the same steps to glue Pop-up B on top of A.

4. Open the pop-up. Apply glue to the pop-up tab on Pop-up A. Place the red paper candle against the tab. Close the pop-up and press firmly again. Allow to dry.

5. Cut a flame from the yellow paper and glue to the candle.

6. Punch 2 holes in the outside edges of the folder. Tie one end of the roving into each hole. Tie the 2 free ends in a bow.

7. Color and cut out the label for the outside of the card. Glue it in place.

Hanukkah Pop-Up Card
PATTERNS

Pop-up A

Happy Hanukkah

Pop-up B

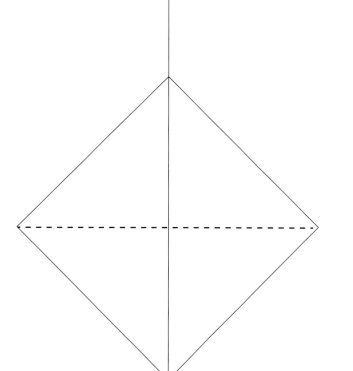

Celebrating Hanukkah,
Add one candle every night.
The menorah spreads a special light.

Art for All Seasons • EMC 2001 • ©2004 by Evan-Moor Corp.

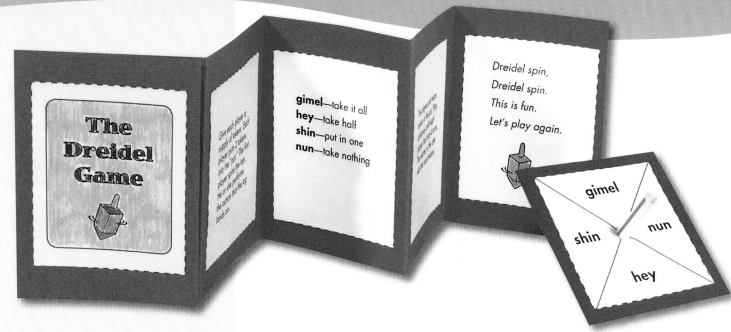

What a great project for students to take home! Each time they teach the game to a friend, they can share the little book and review the rules.

MATERIALS

- patterns on the following page, reproduced for each student
- 4" x 18" (10 x 45.5 cm) blue construction paper for the cover
- 3" (7.5 cm) square of blue construction paper for the top
- 2" (5 cm) piece of a drinking straw
- crayons, marking pens, or colored pencils
- scissors
- glue
- ruler
- hole punch

Spin, Dreidel, Spin Minibook

STEPS TO FOLLOW

1. Accordion-fold the blue construction paper as shown.

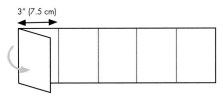

3" (7.5 cm)

2. Color and cut apart the patterns. Glue the title page to the front of the little book. Leave the next panel blank. Then paste the rest of the pages on the remaining panels.

3. Make the top according to the directions on the pattern page.

The Dreidel Game

A dreidel is a four-sided top used to play a game that has been a Hanukkah tradition for hundreds of years.

Give each player a supply of tokens. Each player puts 2 tokens into the "pot." The first player spins the top. He or she performs the action that the top lands on.

gimel—take it all
hey—take half
shin—put in one
nun—take nothing

The players put more tokens in the pot. Play continues until each player has had 4 turns. The winner is the one with the most tokens.

Dreidel spin,
Dreidel spin.
This is fun.
Let's play again.

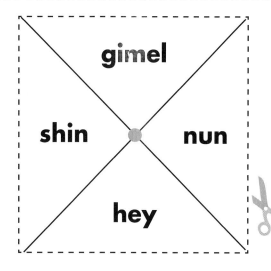

How to make a dreidel top:
1. Cut out the pattern.
2. Glue it to a 3" (7.5 cm) square piece of blue construction paper.
3. Punch a hole in the center.
4. Insert a 2" (5 cm) piece of drinking straw.
5. Spin and play.

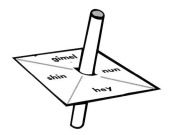

Art for All Seasons • EMC 2001 • ©2004 by Evan-Moor Corp.

These designs are so much fun, students will want to try more than one.

Turnabout Design

MATERIALS

- templates on the following page
- 4—4" x 5" (10 x 12.5 cm) construction paper pieces for the figures
- 9" (23 cm) square of colored construction paper for the base
- scissors
- pencil
- glue
- paint, stickers, marking pens, etc., to use for adding details

STEPS TO FOLLOW

1. Trace the template onto the 4 pieces of construction paper. Cut on the lines.

2. Fold the colored construction paper base into quarters.

3. Lay one pattern piece in each quarter, rotating the base around the center point. The corners or tips of each pattern should just touch. Glue them in place.

4. Add details using your medium of choice.

Stencil once to create a holiday card, or stencil over and over to create wrapping paper. Students will be thrilled with the results of this project.

MATERIALS

- templates of stencil designs on the following page
- 5" x 9" (12.5 x 23 cm) construction paper for the background
- 3" x 7" (7.5 x 18 cm) tagboard for the stencil
- 6" x 9" (15 x 23 cm) construction paper for the frame
- assorted colors of tempera paint
- shallow dishes
- small rectangular sponges—some cut into heart shapes
- pencil
- craft knife
- glue

Stencil It

STEPS TO FOLLOW

1. Trace the stencil pattern onto the tagboard. Cut it out with a craft knife. Make several copies of each stencil. It is best to make one for each color of paint you plan to use.

2. Lay the stencil on the background paper. Pour puddles of paint into shallow dishes. Dip the sponge in the paint and dab it on the stencil. Gently lift off the stencil to see the result. Let the paint dry thoroughly.

3. Add other details to the design, such as a heart sponge print in the center of the O in JOY.

4. Rip around the edge of the stenciled paper to create a torn edging. Then tear the frame paper into 4 strips. Lay them around the edges of the background paper as the frame. Glue in place.

Joy

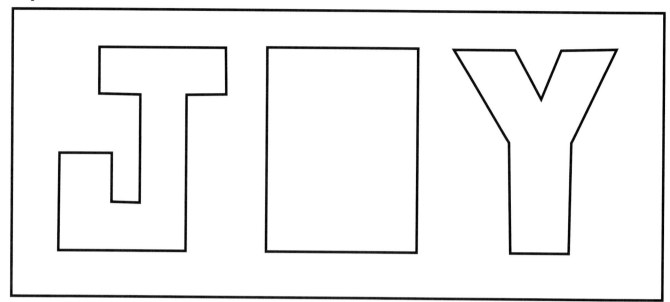

Holly

Star

This activity makes a great gift to send home for the holidays. Santa may be filled with treats or surprises to share.

MATERIALS

- brown paper lunch bag
- 5 ½" (14 cm) square of colorful holiday fabric
- 1 ½" x 5 ½" (4 x 14 cm) strip of fleece
- 6" x 7" (15 x 18 cm) white crepe paper
- 2—1" (2.5 cm) squares of pink construction paper for the cheeks
- 2—1" (2.5 cm) squares of black construction paper for the eyes
- 1" (2.5 cm) square of red construction paper for the nose
- piece of ribbon
- jingle bell

The Santa Bag

STEPS TO FOLLOW

1. Glue the fabric even with the top of the lunch bag. Fold that section in half diagonally.

2. Fold the crepe paper in half. Cut fringe the full length of the paper within ½" (1.25 cm) of the fold.

3. Glue the crepe paper as a beard below where the fabric begins. Trim the beard to fit the bag.

4. Cut black eyes, a red nose, and pink cheeks from the construction paper pieces.

5. Glue the fleece to the bottom of the hat.

6. Tie a ribbon bow on the bell. Glue the bell to the top point of the hat.

Reindeer Card Holder

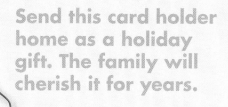

STEPS TO FOLLOW

1. Fold the corners of the white construction paper over the wire hanger and tape in place.

2. Fold up 3" (7.5 cm) of the lower edge of the white paper and tape.

3. Round two corners of the large brown paper for the reindeer's head. Lay it on the holder with the bottom slipped inside the folded-up section.

4. Trace around a child's hand on the black construction paper. Hold the two pieces together and cut on the pencil line. Lay the antlers on the holder. Slip them under the brown head piece.

5. Draw a leaf shape on the brown paper for ears. Hold both pieces together and cut on the line. Fold the ears in half as shown and lay them on the reindeer's head.

6. Lay the piece for the collar where you think it works best.

7. Cut out circles for the eyes and nose and lay in place.

8. Adjust all the pieces you have cut and decide on the arrangement that you like the best. Now glue all the pieces in place.

9. Bend the pieces for the legs to fit in the pocket. Tape the legs in place. Add black hooves cut from paper scraps.

10. Students may decorate the pocket label on the pattern page. Cut it out and glue it to the pocket as shown.

11. Glue on the black beans for the eyes and glue the beads on the collar. Add details using a black marker.

12. Tie a bow on the top of the hanger.

Step 1

Step 2

Step 5

Send this card holder home as a holiday gift. The family will cherish it for years.

MATERIALS

- patterns on the following page, reproduced for each student

- wire hanger

- 12" x 18" (30.5 x 45.5 cm) white construction paper for the holder

- 6" x 12" (15 x 30.5 cm) brown construction paper for the head

- 2—3" x 4" (7.5 x 10 cm) brown construction paper pieces for the ears

- 2—2" x 6" (5 x 15 cm) brown construction paper pieces for the legs

- 2—6" (15 cm) squares of black construction paper for the antlers

- 2½" (6 cm) square of red construction paper for the nose

- 2—1" (2.5 cm) squares of blue construction paper for the eyes

- 1" x 6½" (2.5 x 16.5 cm) green construction paper for the collar

- 2 black beans

- 8 red beads

- festive holiday ribbon

- pencil and marking pen

- tape

Art for All Seasons • EMC 2001 • ©2004 by Evan-Moor Corp.

Pocket Label

Sleigh Time

STEPS TO FOLLOW

1. Fold the brown paper in half. Sketch and cut out a hill shape for the reindeer's head as shown.

2. Cut strips from the black paper for the antlers. Glue them to one of the head pieces.

3. Add eyes and a nose to both of the head pieces using a marking pen and paper scraps.

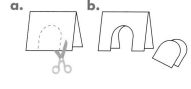

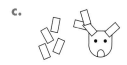

4. Glue the two head pieces back to back around one end of the body. Cut a small tail on the opposite end of the reindeer. Also fold up ½" (1 cm) of each leg. Now the reindeer is ready to go.

5. Fold the red paper in half for the sleigh. Cut out a part on the fold as shown. Trim the edges of the black runner paper and glue to the sleigh. Add other details with a marking pen and paper scraps.

6. Set the reindeer and the sleigh on the blue base to give the impression that they are soaring through the night sky. Add foil stars to the blue paper.

7. Tie the reindeer and sleigh together with a green ribbon.

Students may want to make all of Santa's reindeer after discovering how easy this one is to make. They may also want to add a driver and a big bag of toys to the sleigh.

MATERIALS

- 5" x 8" (12.5 x 20 cm) brown construction paper for the reindeer

- 1" x 2" (2.5 x 5 cm) black construction paper for the antlers

- 6" x 7" (15 x 18 cm) red construction paper for the sleigh

- 1" x 6" (2.5 x 15 cm) black construction paper for the runners

- 4 ½" x 12" (11.5 x 30.5 cm) blue construction paper for the base

- a strip of green roving or ribbon

- paper scraps in assorted colors for details

- foil star stickers

- marking pen

- scissors

- glue

Students may use their three elves in a multitude of ways: on the desk to hold reminders, spelling words, etc.; as a visual to accompany a holiday story; to take home with their Christmas wish list; and so much more.

MATERIALS

- patterns on the following page, reproduced for each student
- 3—6" (15 cm) squares of green construction paper for the elves' bodies
- 6—½" x 3" (1.25 x 7.5 cm) green construction paper strips for the arms
- assorted colors of paper scraps for details
- stapler
- pencil
- glue
- scissors
- crayons, marking pens, or colored pencils

Helpful Little Elves

STEPS TO FOLLOW

1. Fold the basic cross-legged body for each of the elves.

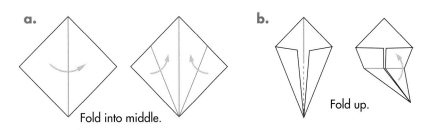

a.

Fold into middle.

b.

Fold up.

c.

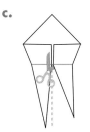

Cut up to the fold.

d.

Cross over the legs and staple. Staple the body and round off.

e.

Roll the toes of the elves on a pencil.

2. Color and cut out the patterns for the heads. Glue them in place.

3. Accordion-fold the green strips for the arms. Glue them to the sides of the cross-legged bodies.

4. Color and cut out the apron patterns. Glue them over the front of each pocket.

5. Cut out the pocket stuffers and store them in the elves' pockets.

Helpful Little Elves
PATTERNS

Heads

Aprons

 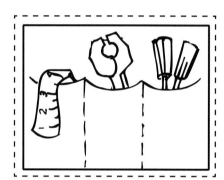 

Pocket Stuffers

  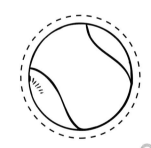

  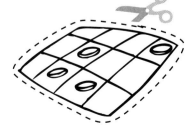

Art for All Seasons • EMC 2001 • ©2004 by Evan-Moor Corp.

Little Drummer Boy

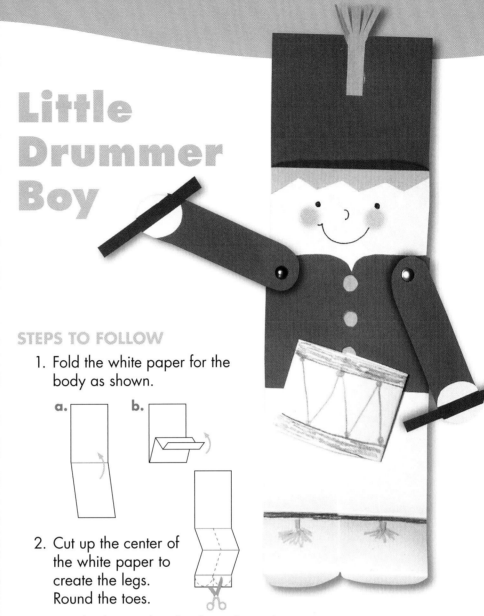

Line up all the students' drummers on your bulletin board. Let students personalize them to look like themselves, and then display student work below.

MATERIALS

- templates on the following page
- 4" x 12" (10 x 30.5 cm) white construction paper for the body
- 6" x 8" (15 x 20 cm) red construction paper for the hat and jacket
- 2 ¼" x 7" (5.5 x 18 cm) white construction paper for the drum
- 2" x 4" (5 x 10 cm) yellow construction paper for the hair and trim
- paper scraps for details
- 2 paper fasteners
- crayons, marking pens, or colored pencils
- glue
- scissors

STEPS TO FOLLOW

1. Fold the white paper for the body as shown.

   a.   b.

2. Cut up the center of the white paper to create the legs. Round the toes.

3. Cut the hat and jacket from the red construction paper using the templates as a guide. Fold up a visor on the hat.

4. Cut the hair from the yellow construction paper using the template as a guide.

5. Glue the hair, jacket, and hat pieces to the body as shown.

6. Cut the arm pieces from red construction paper using the template as a guide.

7. Attach the arms with the paper fasteners.

8. Decorate the drum strip. Roll and glue it into a cylinder. Glue it to the front of the jacket.

9. Cut two hands and drumsticks from paper scraps. Glue them to the arms of the jacket.

10. Add facial features and other details with crayons, marking pens, colored pencils, or paper scraps.

Hat (red)

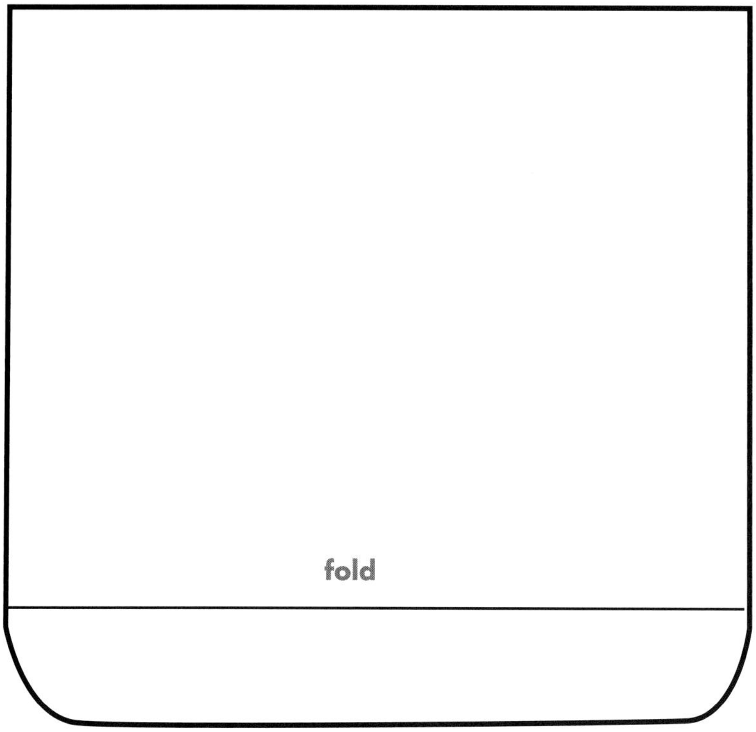

fold

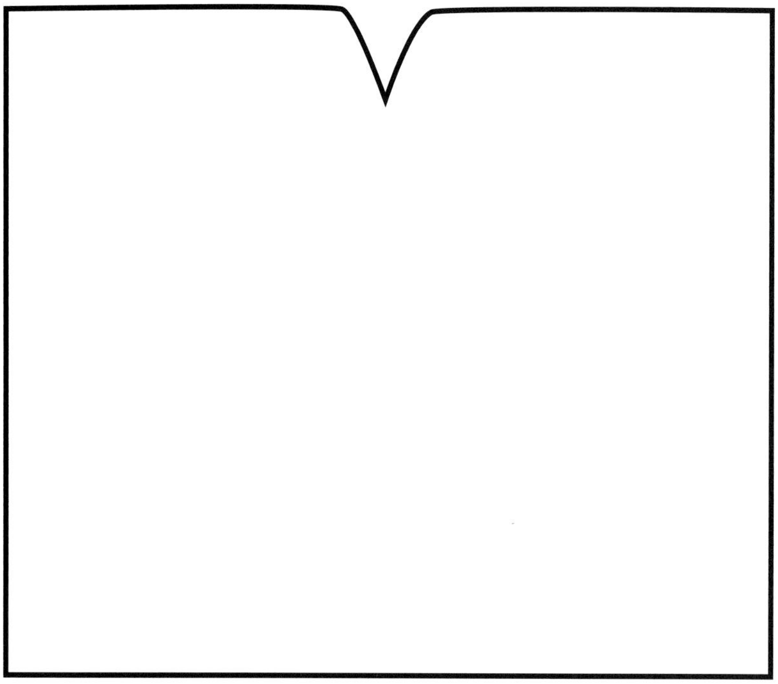

Hair (yellow)

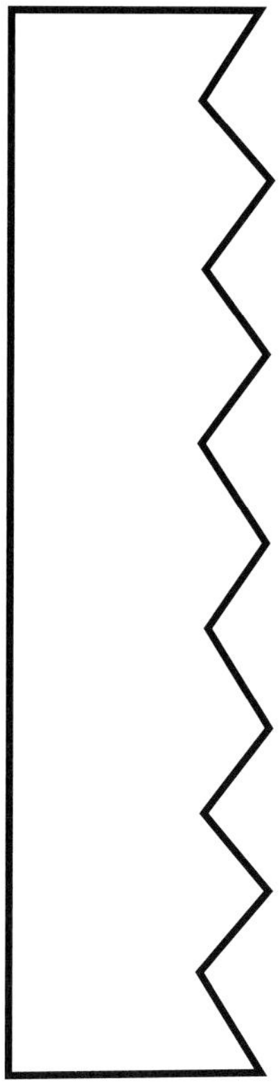

Arm (red—Cut 2)

Jacket (red)

Hand (white—Cut 2)

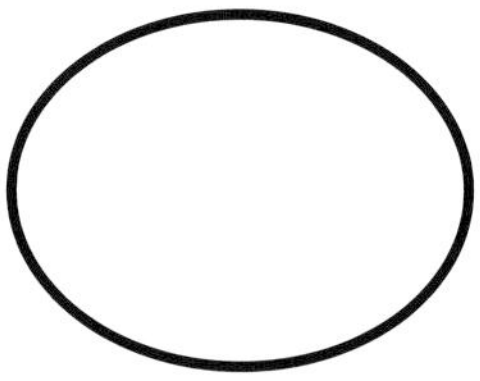

Art for All Seasons • EMC 2001 • ©2004 by Evan-Moor Corp.

This easy-to-make angel has so many uses—as a bulletin board border, a tree ornament, or a decoration for the holiday table.

MATERIALS

- patterns on the following 2 pages, reproduced for each student
- 8" (20 cm) square of pink construction paper for the body
- 5" x 9" (12.5 x 23 cm) white construction paper for the head and arms
- crayons, marking pens, or colored pencils
- glue
- double-stick tape
- scissors
- paper fastener
- hole punch
- length of ribbon or yarn

A Christmas Angel

STEPS TO FOLLOW

1. Color and cut out the patterns.

2. Glue the body pattern to the center of the pink construction paper. Trim around the edge, leaving a pink rim visible.

3. Glue the head and arms pattern to the white construction paper. Trim around the outside edge close to the pattern.

4. Cut on the dotted line into the center of the body pattern. Fold on the designated lines.

5. Place a strip of double-stick tape along the fold line on the wings. Roll the body into a cone shape and let the tape stick the wings together. Roll the tips of the wings out.

6. Use a paper fastener to attach the head and arms to the body.

7. Use double-stick tape to secure the candle in one hand.

8. Punch a hole in the back. Tie a ribbon through the hole to use as a hanger.

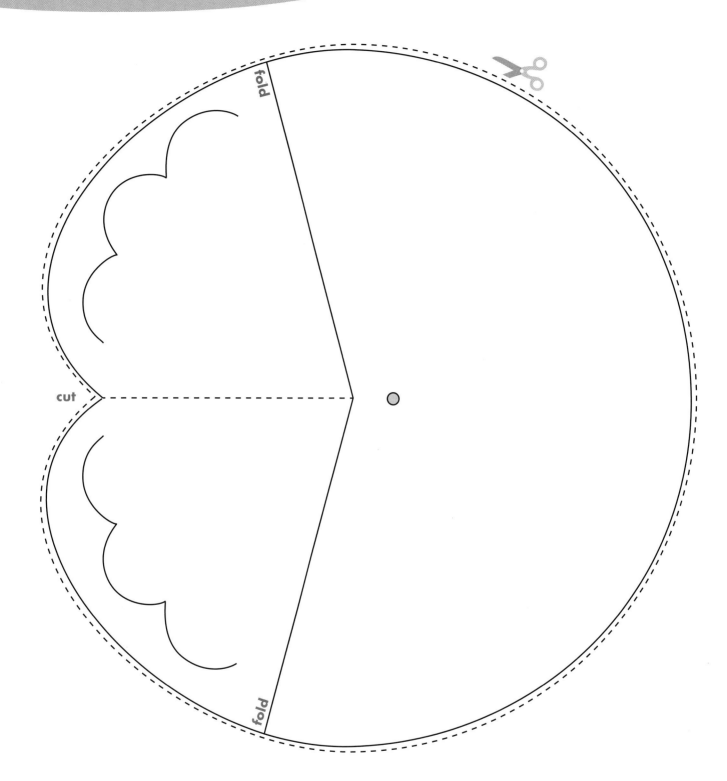

fold

cut

fold

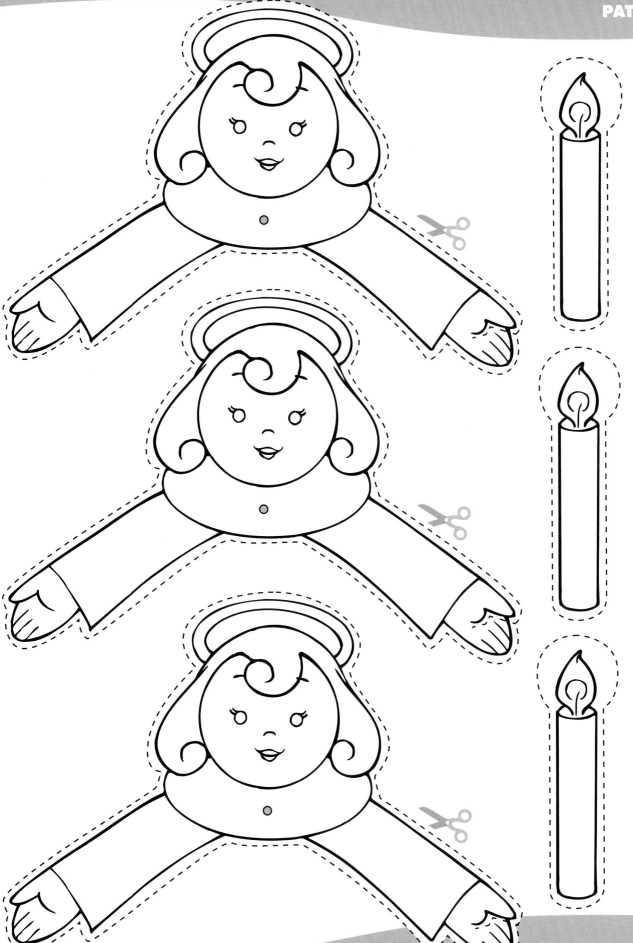

My Santa Paper Doll

STEPS TO FOLLOW

1. Color and cut out the Santa pattern. Glue it to the black backing paper. Trim around the edges.

2. Color an outfit for the jolly fellow using the patterns provided.

3. Cut out the clothing and try it on him.

4. Fold the green folder paper in half and then fold up the bottom 2″ (5 cm). Glue the label provided to the front. Slip Santa and his outfits inside and tuck them away for a later time.

Is Santa relaxing at the North Pole or carrying out his Christmas deliveries? Students dress Santa as they wish, even creating their own designs.

MATERIALS

- patterns on the following 3 pages, reproduced for each student

- 8″ x 10″ (20 x 25.5 cm) black construction paper for the backing

- 12″ x 18″ (30.5 x 45.5 cm) green construction paper for the folder cover

- crayons, marking pens, or colored pencils

- scissors

- glue

Art for All Seasons • EMC 2001 • ©2004 by Evan-Moor Corp.

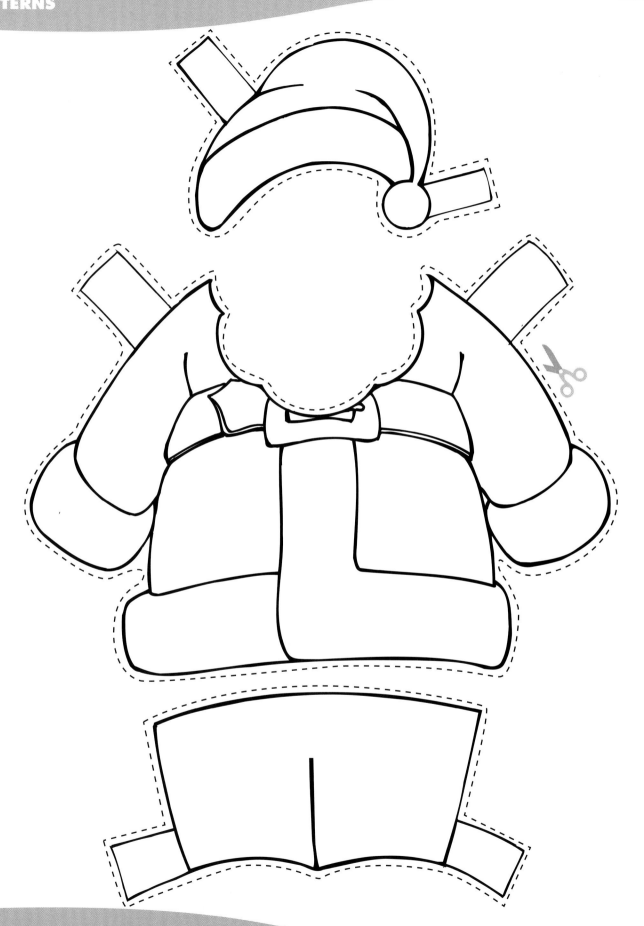

Folder Label

My Santa Paper Doll

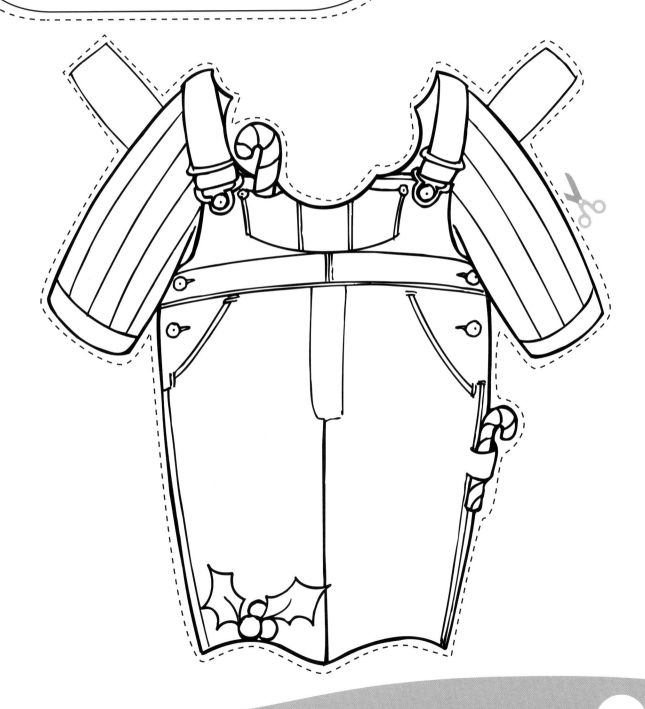

MATERIALS

- fingers
- white construction paper cut to desired sizes for base of card
- colored construction paper cut to frame card
- red, green, and blue ink pads
- crayons, marking pens, or colored pencils
- red and yellow tempera paint
- pencil with a new eraser
- glue
- scissors
- yarn or ribbon

Festive Fingerprint Art Cards

STEPS TO FOLLOW

1. Experiment with using fingers as a print tool. Stamp designs on practice paper to experiment with how hard to press, etc.

2. Fold the paper in half for the card.

3. Create the fingerprint design on the front cover.

4. Use a pencil eraser dipped in tempera paint to add details.

5. Use the crayons, marking pens, or colored pencils to add a greeting inside.

6. Glue the card onto complementary-colored construction paper to add color.

7. Add yarn as a finishing touch.

These candy canes are so much fun, you'll want to make lots of them. Hang them on a Christmas tree; use them on a bulletin board; tie them to a gift. The uses go on and on.

MATERIALS

- 8" (20 cm) square of white construction paper
- 7" (18 cm) square of white construction paper
- 6" (15 cm) square of white construction paper
- red crayon
- tape
- pencil
- ribbon

The Most Remarkable Candy Cane

STEPS TO FOLLOW

1. Color a red stripe along two outer edges of the white paper. Flip the paper over.

2. Beginning at the corner **opposite** the colored edges, roll the paper around a pencil. Keep rolling until the paper is completely rolled up. The real fun is seeing the candy-cane effect develop as you roll the paper.

3. Tape down the end point of the paper.

4. Flatten one end of the candy cane. Now roll that over the pencil to create the hooked end.

5. Tie a ribbon around the candy cane.

Flip the paper over.

The seven candles of the kinara symbolize positive values. Summarize your study of Kwanzaa with his project.

A Kinara for Kwan aa

MATERIALS

- patterns on the following page, reproduced for each student
- 9" x 12" (23 x 30.5 cm) yellow construction paper for the base
- 1" x 4" (2.5 x 10 cm) green, red, and black construction paper strips for the candles
- 2" x 4" (5 x 10 cm) yellow construction paper for the flames
- ruler
- crayons, marking pens, or colored pencils
- scissors
- glue
- stapler

STEPS TO FOLLOW

1. Fold the yellow paper in half. Then fold up a 2" (5 cm) strip on both outer ends. Refold the flaps to the inside. This is the base of the kinara.

2. Color and cut out the patterns.

3. Glue the Kwanzaa label in the lower section of the folded yellow paper. Glue the list of the seven principles to the back.

4. Arrange the candle strips above the Kwanzaa label in color order: 3 green, 1 black, and 3 red. Glue in place.

5. Cut out and glue yellow flames for the candles.

6. Stand up the kinara. Staple the 2 flaps at the base, overlapping each other slightly to create a stand.

Art for All Seasons • EMC 2001 • ©2004 by Evan-Moor Corp.

Front Panel

Kwanzaa

Back Panel

The seven candles on the kinara represent the seven principles of Kwanzaa:

- unity
- self-determination
- collective work and responsibility
- cooperative economics
- purpose
- creativity
- faith

Front Panel

Kwanzaa

Back Panel

The seven candles on the kinara represent the seven principles of Kwanzaa:

- unity
- self-determination
- collective work and responsibility
- cooperative economics
- purpose
- creativity
- faith

Chinese New Year Dragon

Celebrate Chinese New Year with a dragon parade in your classroom. Students wear their own dragon headband and welcome the new year as they march around the room.

MATERIALS

- templates on the following page
- 10" x 18" (25.5 x 45.5 cm) green construction paper for the headband
- 2—2" x 5" (5 x 12.5 cm) pieces of green construction paper for the ears
- 2—1 ½" x 2" (4 x 5 cm) pieces of white construction paper for the eyes
- 2—1" (2.5 cm) squares of black construction paper for the pupils
- 2—3" (7.5 cm) squares of red construction paper for the nostrils
- 2—2 ½" x 3" (6 x 7.5 cm) pieces of yellow construction paper for the horns
- pencil
- scissors
- glue

STEPS TO FOLLOW

1. Sketch a zigzag line on the green headband paper. Cut on that line.

2. Fit the headband strip to the child's head. Remove and staple the end in place. Let the left-over section stick out.

3. Set the headband on the table and decide where the face of the dragon will best fit. Use the templates to help cut out the pieces.
   a. Round the corners on the white paper for the eyes.
   b. Cut circles from the black pieces for the pupils.
   c. Cut ear shapes from the green paper. Fold down a flap on the end.
   d. Cut spirals from the red paper for nostrils.
   e. Cut horns from the yellow paper.

4. Glue all the pieces in place.

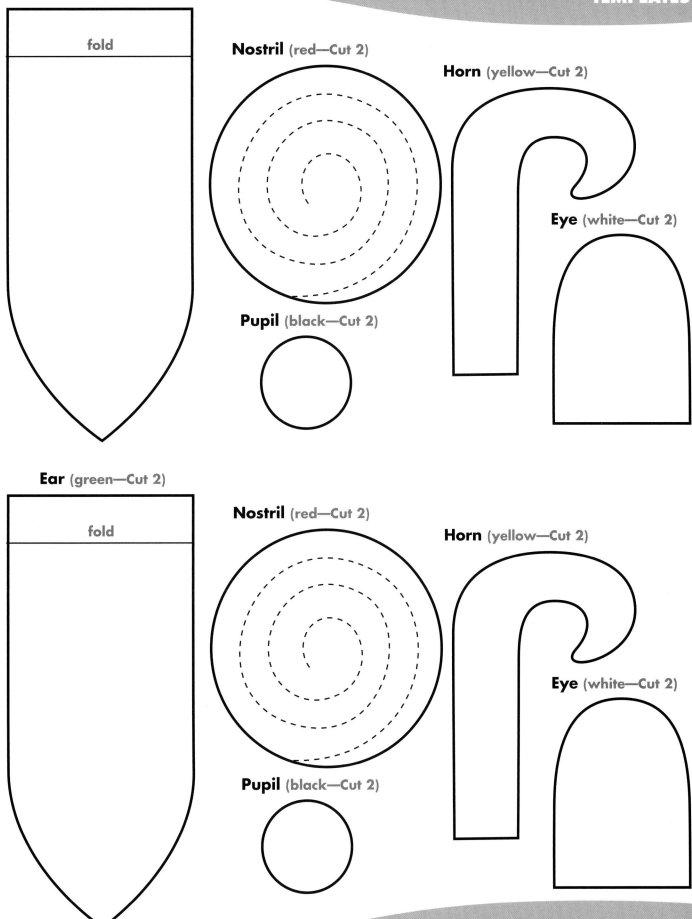

Ear (green—Cut 2)

fold

Nostril (red—Cut 2)

Horn (yellow—Cut 2)

Eye (white—Cut 2)

Pupil (black—Cut 2)

Ear (green—Cut 2)

fold

Nostril (red—Cut 2)

Horn (yellow—Cut 2)

Eye (white—Cut 2)

Pupil (black—Cut 2)

Mr. Groundhog

Out of his tunnel
From the earth below,
Up pops Mr. Groundhog!
Ask him what he knows.

Will we have sunshine?
Will there be more snow?
Ask Mr. Groundhog.
Only he will know.

Howdy, Groundhog

STEPS TO FOLLOW

1. Fold up 4" (10 cm) of the green paper. Round the corners of the folded section.

2. Use the craft knife to cut a 2" (5 cm) slit in the center of the fold line on the green paper.

3. Glue the blue paper sky in place inside the green folded paper.

4. Round the corners of the yellow square to make the sun. Lay it on the blue paper.

5. Cut out the patterns.

6. Lay the cloud pattern over the sun. Adjust both and glue in place.

7. Trace around the groundhog template onto the brown construction paper. Cut it out and add details with paper scraps and marking pens, crayons, or colored pencils.

8. Tape the groundhog to the straw and insert it in the slit.

9. Staple the folder shut.

10. Glue the poem to the front of the folder.

11. Have the students move their groundhog around as the poem is read.

a. b.

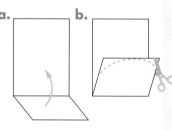

c.

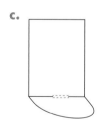

Steps 8 & 9

a. b.

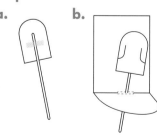

c.

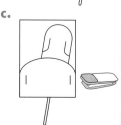

This pop-up puppet is a memorable way to celebrate Groundhog Day. It can be a great motivator for a writing assignment.

MATERIALS

- patterns and templates on the following page

- 6" x 12" (15 x 30.5 cm) green construction paper for the background/folder

- 5" x 7" (12.5 x 18 cm) blue construction paper for the sky

- 3" x 4" (7.5 x 10 cm) brown construction paper for the groundhog

- 2" (5 cm) square of yellow construction paper for the sun

- paper scraps

- craft knife

- crayons, marking pens, or colored pencils

- straw

- tape

- stapler

- scissors

- glue

- ruler

Groundhog (brown)

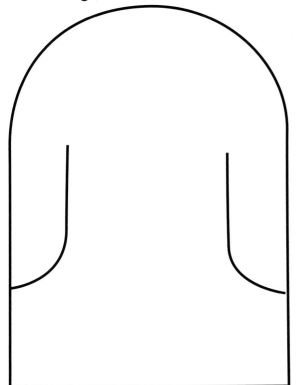

Poem

Mr. Groundhog

Out of his tunnel
From the earth below,
Up pops Mr. Groundhog!
Ask him what he knows.

Will we have sunshine?
Will there be more snow?
Ask Mr. Groundhog.
Only he will know.

Cloud

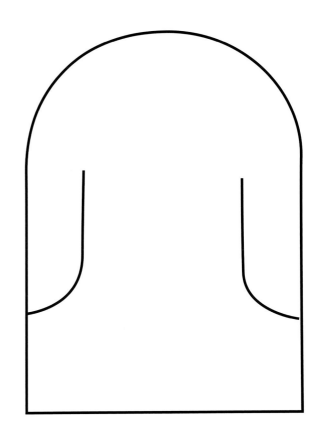

Sun

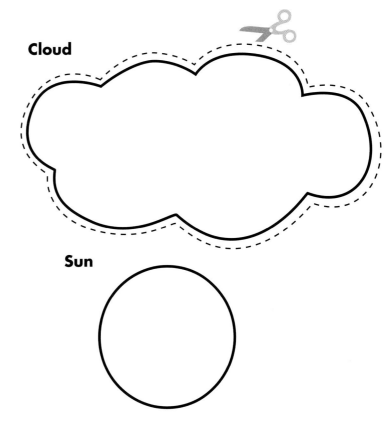

A Woven Valentine Card

STEPS TO FOLLOW

1. Trace around the templates on the construction paper.
2. Cut the slits as indicated.
3. Fold the double piece on the fold line.
4. Weave the two sections together as shown.
5. Glue the end pieces to secure.
6. Cut a small heart from scraps of paper. Glue it and the message inside the card.

Make these cards using different colors of construction paper. Students are fascinated by the process and enjoy experimenting with color variations.

MATERIALS

- templates and pattern on the following page
- 6" x 12" (15 x 30.5 cm) white or pink construction paper
- 4" x 6" (10 x 15 cm) red or purple construction paper
- scissors
- glue
- pencil

Message

Happy
Valentine's
Day

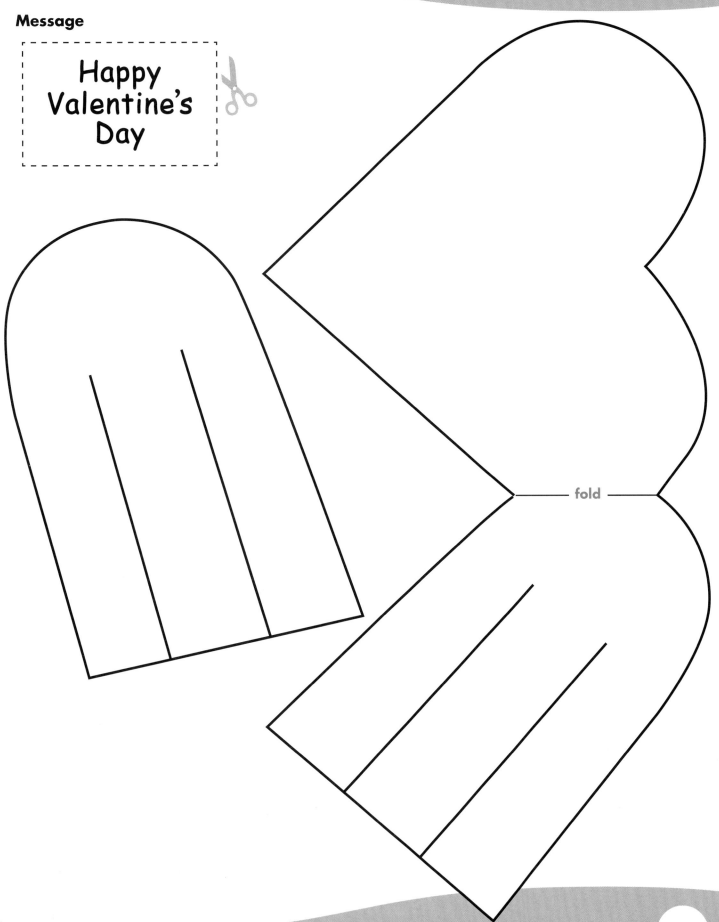

fold

A Heart Basket

These little baskets created from two circles of construction paper are easy to make. Make them in any color combination and in various sizes.

STEPS TO FOLLOW

1. Fold the construction paper squares in half. Round the corners.

2. Place one folded circle inside the other to form a right angle. Glue them in that position to form the basket.

3. Punch holes to form a pattern on the handle.

4. Glue the handle to the basket.

5. Write a Valentine's message on the scroll paper. Roll it up and secure it with a piece of ribbon or yarn.

MATERIALS

- 2—4" (10 cm) squares in various colors appropriate to the holiday

- 1" x 8" (2.5 x 20 cm) construction paper for the handle

- 4" (10 cm) square of copy paper for the scroll

- hole punch

- scissors

- glue

- yarn or ribbon

Art for All Seasons • EMC 2001 • ©2004 by Evan-Moor Corp.

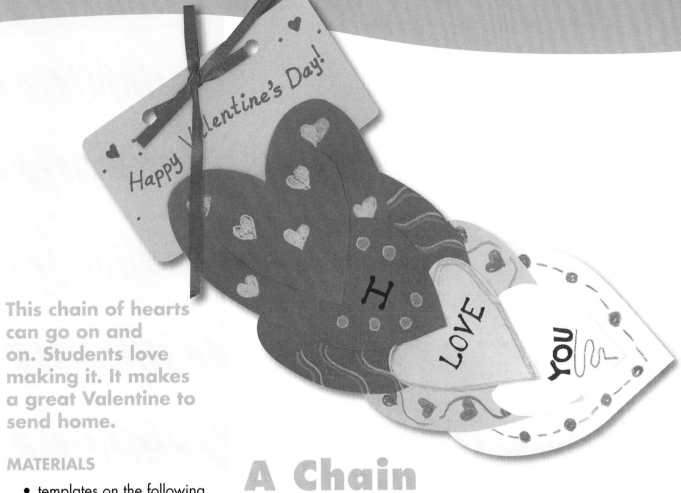

This chain of hearts can go on and on. Students love making it. It makes a great Valentine to send home.

MATERIALS

- templates on the following page
- 5" (12.5 cm) square of construction paper for each heart in the chain
- 2 ½" x 4 ½" (6 x 11 cm) construction paper for the top piece
- red ribbon
- hole punch
- scissors
- pencil
- crayons, marking pens, or colored pencils
- glue

A Chain of Hearts

STEPS TO FOLLOW

1. Fold each square of construction paper in half. Lay the outer heart template on the fold and trace a light pencil line around it. Cut on the line.

2. Place the inner heart on the fold. Repeat the process for each heart.

3. Open the hearts and decorate them with crayons, marking pens, or colored pencils.

4. Interlock the hearts to form a chain.

5. Write a caption and decorate the top piece. Round the corners.

6. Glue the top of the first heart to the top piece.

7. Punch 2 holes in the top piece and insert ribbon. Tie it in a bow.

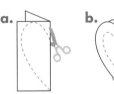

A Chain of Hearts
TEMPLATES

Outer Heart

Inner Heart

Don't cut

place on fold

Outer Heart

Inner Heart

Don't cut

place on fold

Outer Heart

Inner Heart

Don't cut

place on fold

Outer Heart

Inner Heart

Don't cut

place on fold

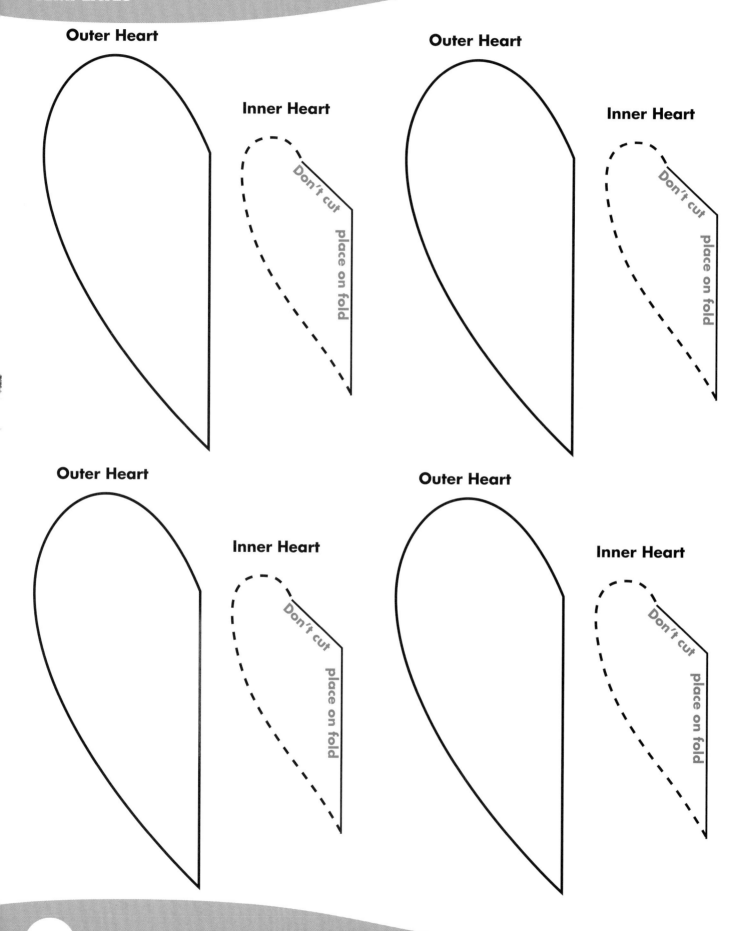

Art for All Seasons • EMC 2001 • ©2004 by Evan-Moor Corp.

These bookmarks can double as Valentine cards for friends. Whether given away or kept, they will be cherished!

MATERIALS

- templates on the following page
- 3″ x 8″ (7.5 x 20 cm) red construction paper for the hearts
- pink scraps of construction paper
- black marking pen
- 8″ (20 cm) length of ribbon
- scissors
- tape
- pencil

My Valentine Bookmark

STEPS TO FOLLOW

1. Trace the templates on the red paper. You will have 3 hearts, each a different size.

2. Cut out the 3 hearts.

3. Add details with pink paper scraps and a marking pen. Fold the ears forward.

4. Lay the hearts on the strip of ribbon. Tape the back of each heart to the ribbon.

5. Use the bookmark to save your place in your favorite storybook.

Body

Head

Tail

Body

Head

Tail

Body

Head

Tail

Art for All Seasons • EMC 2001 • ©2004 by Evan-Moor Corp.

This art lesson also provides basic facts about the life of our 16th president.

MATERIALS

- patterns on the following 2 pages, reproduced for each student
- 9" x 12" (23 x 30.5 cm) red construction paper for the background
- 10" x 13" (25.5 x 33 cm) blue construction paper for the frame
- 5" x 7" (12.5 x 18 cm) black construction paper for the jacket
- 1" x 12" (2.5 x 30.5 cm) strip of black construction paper for the hair
- scissors
- glue
- crayons, marking pens, or colored pencils

A Portrait of Abraham Lincoln

STEPS TO FOLLOW

1. Color and cut out the patterns for Mr. Lincoln's head, collar, and bow tie.
2. Round 2 corners of the black paper for the jacket.
3. Lay the patterns and the jacket on the red paper. Fold down the top of the collar over the bow tie. Glue in place. Begin gluing at the bottom.
4. Rip pieces off the black strip of paper to glue on for Mr. Lincoln's hair and beard.
5. Glue the red paper to the blue paper frame.
6. Color and complete the time line of Mr. Lincoln's life and glue it to the back of his portrait.

Bow tie

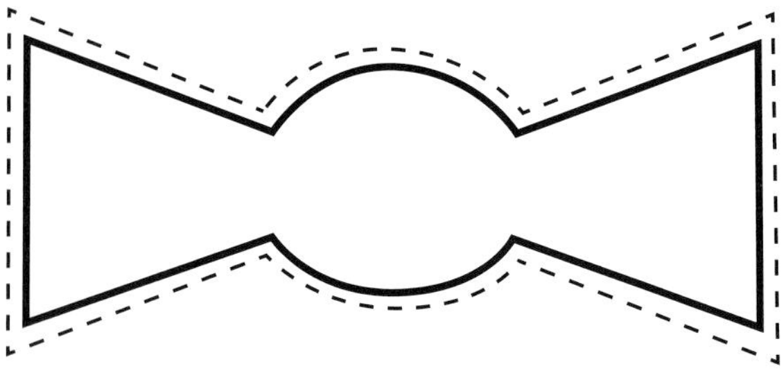

Collar

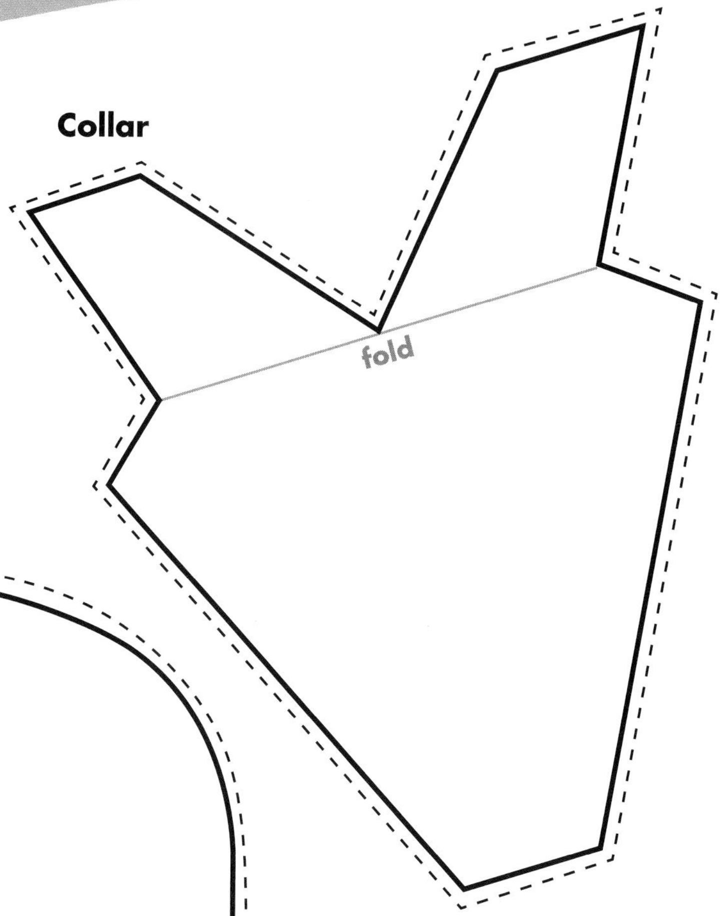

fold

Head

Abraham Lincoln
Time Line

- Abraham Lincoln was born in Kentucky in 1809.

- He moved with his family to Illinois when he was 21.

- He studied to become a lawyer.

- He was elected to the state legislature in 1834.

- In 1842, he married Mary Todd.

- He was elected to Congress in 1846.

- He was elected as our 16th president in 1860.

- He was assasinated in 1865.

A Portrait of George Washington

Our first president never looked better. Students will learn important facts about Mr. Washington's life, too.

MATERIALS

- patterns and template on the following page
- 9" x 12" (23 x 30.5 cm) red construction paper for the background
- 10" x 13" (25.5 x 33 cm) black construction paper for the frame
- 4" x 8" (10 x 20 cm) blue construction paper for the jacket
- 3" x 8" (7.5 x 20 cm) black construction paper for the hat
- 2—1" x 2" (2.5 x 5 cm) pieces of yellow construction paper for the epaulets
- 2 cotton balls
- scissors
- glue
- crayons, marking pens, or colored pencils
- pencil

STEPS TO FOLLOW

1. Color and cut out the patterns for Mr. Washington's face and collar.
2. Round 2 corners of the blue paper for the jacket.
3. Trace around the hat template on the black paper. Cut on the lines.
4. Lay all the pieces on the red paper. Glue in place. Begin gluing at the bottom.
5. Fringe the two pieces of yellow paper for the shoulder epaulets. Glue in place.
6. Pull out the 2 cotton balls and glue to the sides of his face.
7. Cut out other details from scraps of paper and add to the portrait.
8. Glue the red paper to the black paper frame.
9. Color and complete the time line of Mr. Washington's life and glue it to the back of his portrait.

Art for All Seasons • EMC 2001 • ©2004 by Evan-Moor Corp.

Face

Hat (black)

Collar

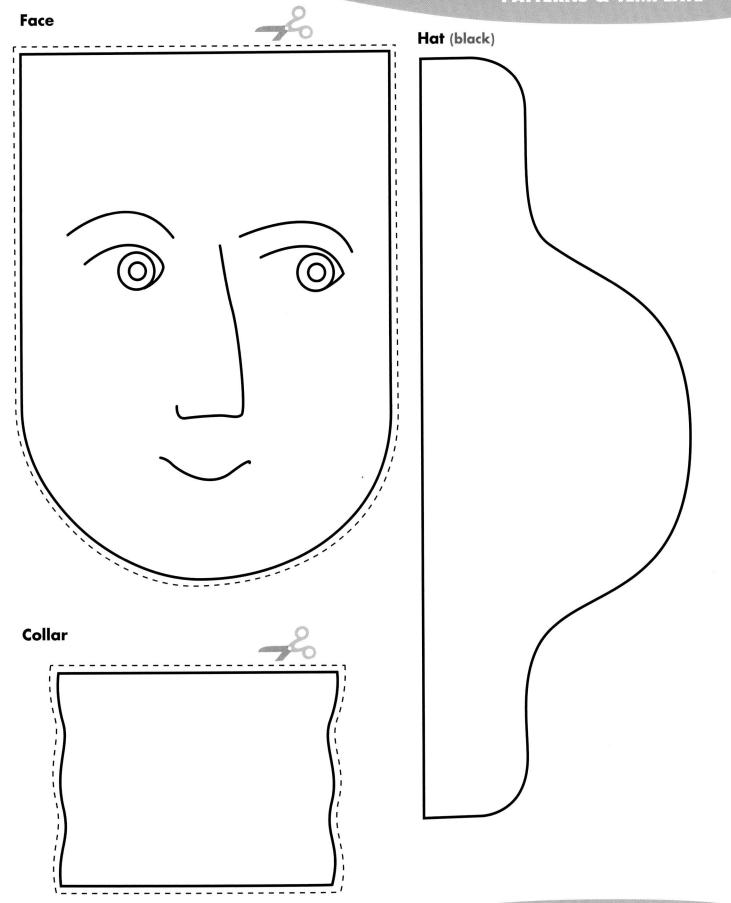

George Washington Time Line

- George Washington was born in Virginia in 1732.

- He lived during the Colonial period.

- He had many adventures as a surveyor and a soldier.

- He married Martha Curtis in 1759, and their home was at Mount Vernon.

- In 1775, he became a general in the Revolutionary War.

- He became our first president in 1789.

- George Washington died in 1799.

Contents

Slicker Kid

There is nothing like a yellow slicker to brighten a rainy day. This Slicker Kid has movable arms. Display him in various positions on a bulletin board as a motivator for rainy day stories.

STEPS TO FOLLOW

1. Use the templates to cut out the body parts from construction paper: yellow—slicker, arms, and hat; red—umbrella and boots; white—head and hands.

2. Lay all the parts on the table to see how they match up. Add the blue pieces for the pant legs.

3. Punch holes as indicated on the slicker and arms.

4. Attach the arms to the main body of the slicker with the paper fasteners.

5. Glue the rest of the pieces together.

6. Create a handle for the umbrella by inserting the straw through the holes punched in the right hand and the umbrella.

7. Add details with crayons, marking pens, or colored pencils.

MATERIALS

- templates on the following 2 pages
- 6" x 12" (15 x 30.5 cm) yellow construction paper for the slicker, arms, and hat
- 5" x 7" (12.5 x 18 cm) red construction paper for the umbrella and boots
- 2—2" x 2½" (5 x 6 cm) pieces of blue construction paper for the pant legs
- 5" x 7" (12.5 x 18 cm) white construction paper for the head and hands
- 2 paper fasteners
- drinking straw
- hole punch
- scissors
- glue
- crayons, marking pens, or colored pencils

Umbrella (red)

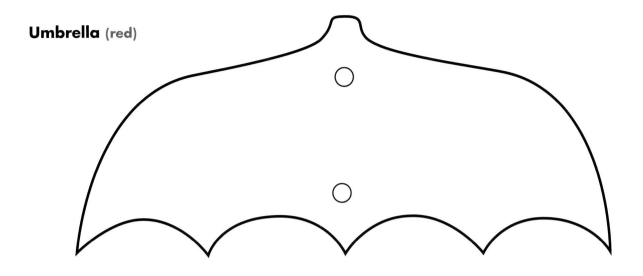

Slicker (yellow)

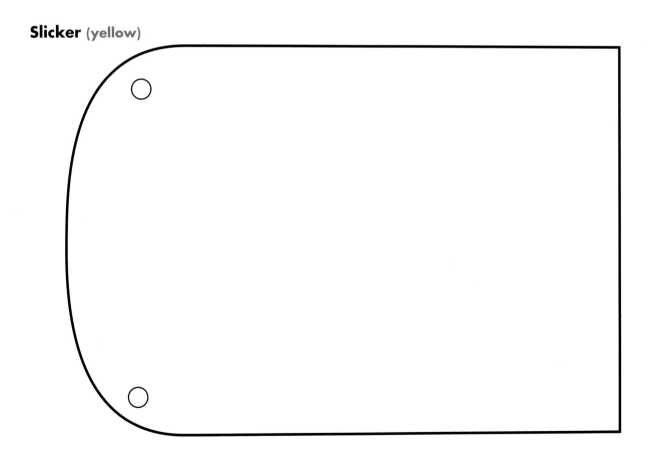

Slicker Kid
TEMPLATES

Head (white)

Hat (yellow)

Hands (white)

Arms (yellow—Cut 2)

Boots (red—Cut 2)

Legs (blue—Cut 2)

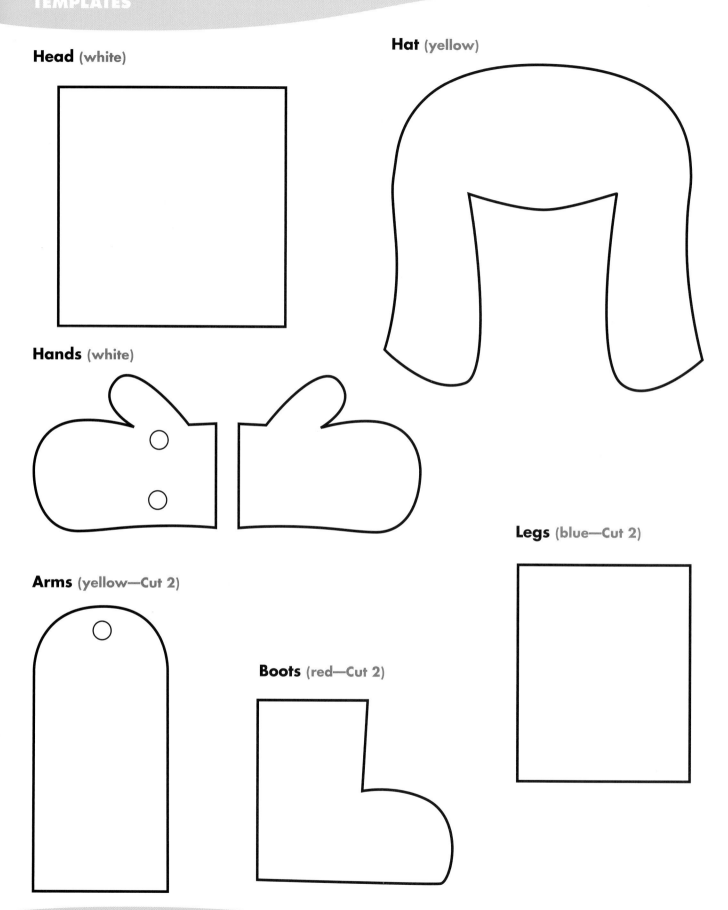

On a warm spring day, young students will love "flying" their butterflies on the playground.

The Butterfly Flyer

MATERIALS

- templates on the following page
- 5" x 8" (12.5 x 20 cm) pieces of construction paper in blue, yellow, and pink for the butterflies
- 3" (7.5 cm) squares of black construction paper for the antennae
- drinking straw
- 1 yard (0.9 m) of clear plastic fishing line
- tape
- hole punch
- scissors
- glue

STEPS TO FOLLOW

1. Use the templates to cut out the butterfly shapes from blue, yellow, and pink paper. Also cut 2 each of the large and small circles from each color.

2. Lay out the 3 butterflies and position the spots so there are contrasting colors on each one as shown.

3. Punch 2 holes in each butterfly as marked on the templates.

4. Cut strips from the black paper for antennae. Fold in half and glue to the butterflies.

5. Thread the fishing line through the straw. Secure it on one end with tape.

6. Now thread the line through the first butterfly (on top) as shown. Tape the line on the back of the butterfly. Repeat this process for the other 2 butterflies. Tape the end of the fishing line to the back of the last butterfly.

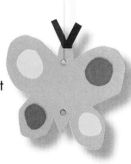

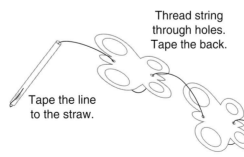

Thread string through holes. Tape the back.

Tape the line to the straw.

Tape the end.

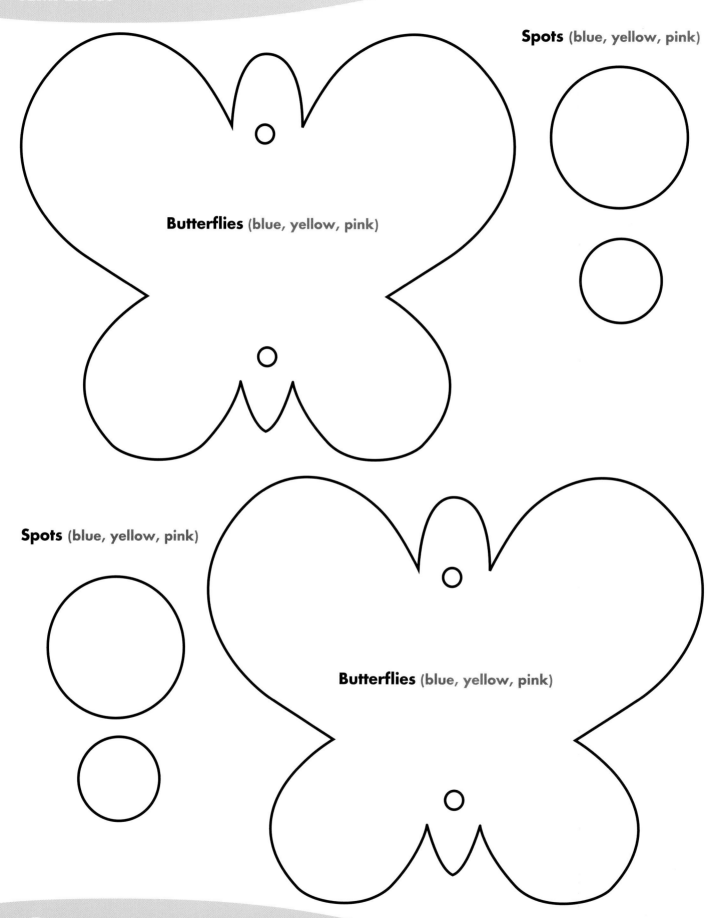

Spots (blue, yellow, pink)

Butterflies (blue, yellow, pink)

Spots (blue, yellow, pink)

Butterflies (blue, yellow, pink)

Raindrops turn into showers to create a graphic portrayal of the old saying—April showers bring May flowers.

MATERIALS

- templates on the following page
- 9" x 12" (23 x 30.5 cm) dark blue construction paper for the background
- 10" x 13" (25.5 x 33 cm) orange construction paper for the frame
- several 3" (7.5 cm) square pieces of white copy paper for raindrop/flowers
- sponges cut into 1" (2.5 cm) squares
- white tempera paint
- shallow dish
- scissors
- glue
- crayons, marking pens, or colored pencils

April Showers

STEPS TO FOLLOW

1. Use the template as a guide to lightly sketch a line delineating the cloud area. Dab the sponges in the white paint and paint in that area. Set it aside to dry.

2. Use colored pencils, crayons, or marking pens to print "April showers bring May flowers" along the bottom of the blue paper.

3. Fold the white copy paper squares as shown. Round the corners.

4. Now you have a raindrop shape. Open it up. The raindrop is transformed into a flower! Color the flower.

5. Make several raindrops that open into flowers and glue them in the blue area.

6. Glue the blue sheet to the orange frame.

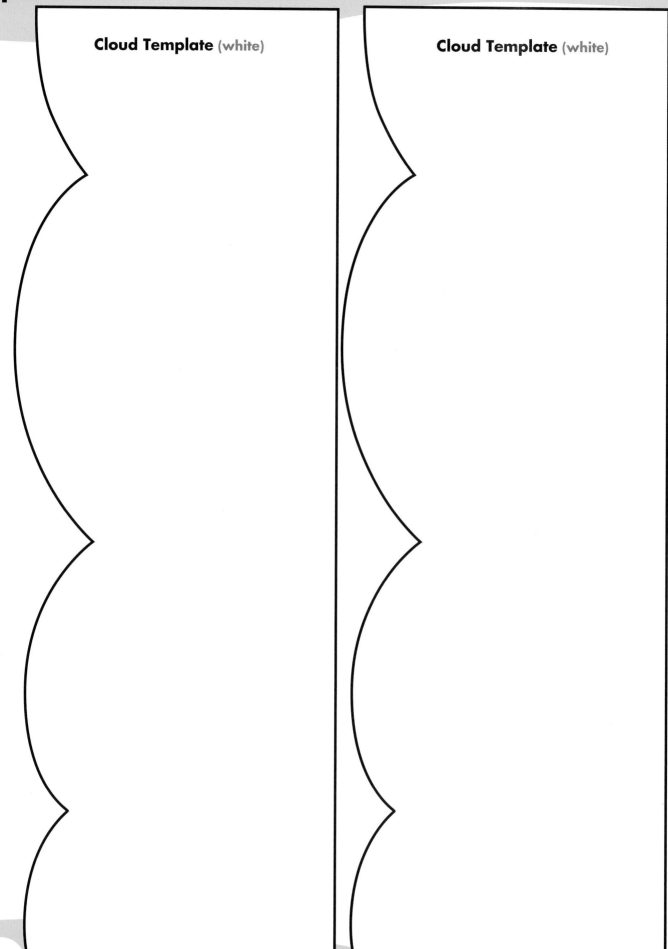

Cloud Template (white)

Cloud Template (white)

Bring pots of red geraniums into the classroom to inspire students before beginning this project. Students of all ages enjoy this project. Challenge older students by having them cut the flowers and leaves free form.

MATERIALS

- templates on the following page
- 9" x 12" (23 x 30.5 cm) dark blue construction paper for the background
- 9 ½" x 12 ½" (24 x 31.5 cm) yellow construction paper for the frame
- 2—5" (12.5 cm) squares of white construction paper for the geraniums
- 4—3 ½" (9 cm) squares of green construction paper for the leaves and stems
- red tempera paint
- pencil
- shallow dish
- glue
- scissors

Fingerprint Geraniums

STEPS TO FOLLOW

1. Trace around the flower template twice on the white paper.

2. Dip a finger into the red paint. Fill the flower shapes with fingerprints. Cut out the flower shapes after the paint is dry.

3. Using the template as a guide, trace around and cut out 3 leaves on the green paper.

4. Cut the last green square into narrow strips to use as stems.

5. Lay out the leaves and stems to establish a design. Glue in place.

6. Glue the blue paper to the yellow frame.

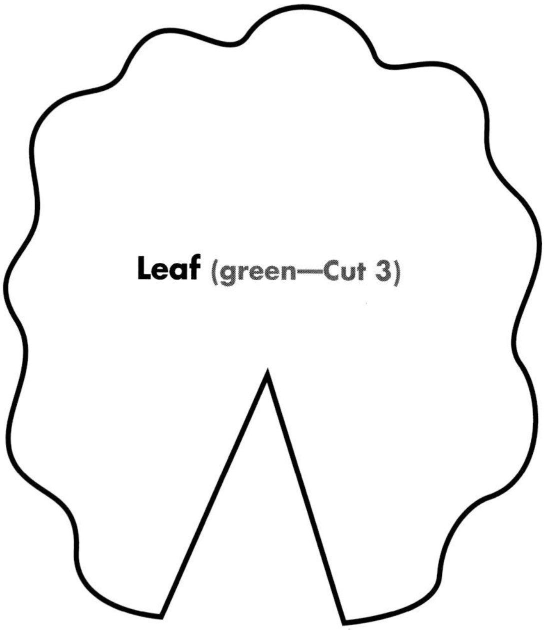

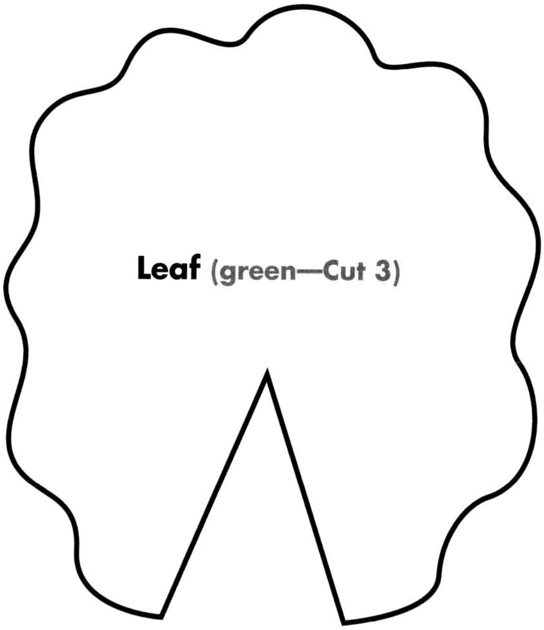

Leaf (green—Cut 3)

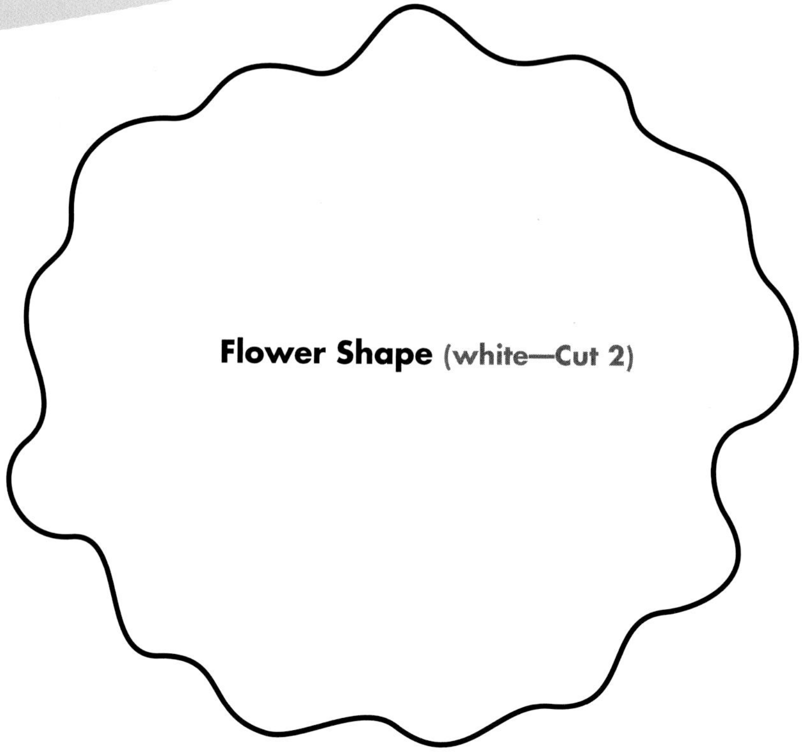

Flower Shape (white—Cut 2)

Leaf (green—Cut 3)

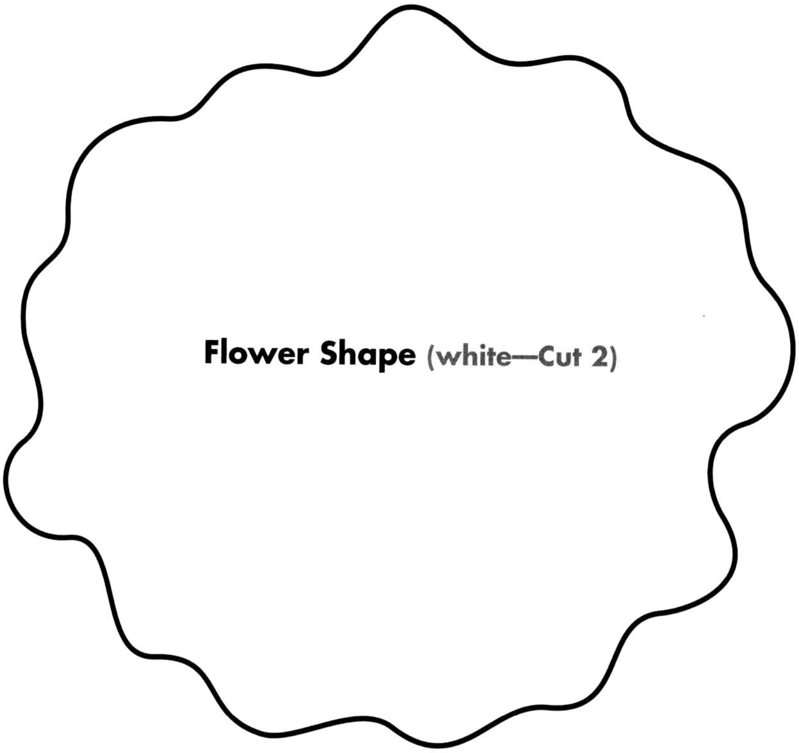

Flower Shape (white—Cut 2)

This quick and easy project will brighten up your room in a jiffy.

MATERIALS

- templates and patterns on the following page
- 4" x 8 ½" (10 x 21.5 cm) pieces of yellow and blue construction paper for the birds' bodies
- 3" (7.5 cm) squares of the same yellow and blue construction paper for the birds' heads
- 6" x 7 ½" (15 x 19 cm) orange construction paper
- plastic drinking straw
- 2—30" (76 cm) lengths of clear plastic fishing line
- hole punch
- pencil
- scissors
- glue
- crayons, marking pens, or colored pencils

Birds bring a message of spring,
In every little song they sing.

Bird Mobile

STEPS TO FOLLOW

1. Fold the blue and yellow construction paper for the bodies as shown.

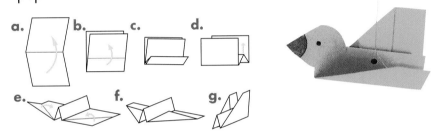

a.   b.   c.   d.

e.   f.   g.

2. Trace around the template provided for the birds' heads on the blue and yellow squares. Cut them out and fold as indicated.

3. Draw beaks and eyes.

4. Glue the heads to the bodies.

5. Punch a hole in the center of the back of each bird.

6. Tie one end of one length of fishing line through the hole punched in the yellow bird. Tie a knot. Thread the other end of that line through the straw and tie it through the hole punched in the blue bird.

7. Thread the other length of fishing line through the straw, too. Tie the two ends together. This forms a loop for hanging the mobile.

8. Fold the orange construction paper in half. Lay it over the straw. Glue the paper shut to secure it around the straw.

9. Cut out and color the poem on the pattern page. Glue it to the orange construction paper.

10. The mobile is now ready to hang.

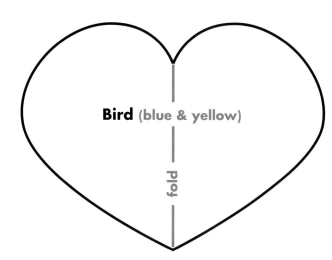
Bird (blue & yellow)

fold

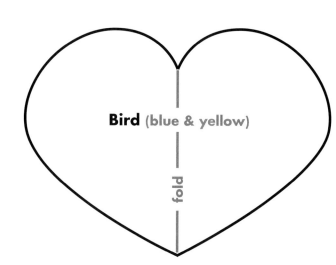
Bird (blue & yellow)

fold

Birds bring a message of spring,
In every little song they sing.

Birds bring a message of spring,
In every little song they sing.

This "flip-around" puppet illustrates the old saying—In like a lion, out like a lamb.

MATERIALS

- patterns and template on the following page
- 2—7" (18 cm) paper plates, 1 yellow and 1 white
- 2 ½" x 4" (6 x 10 cm) yellow construction paper for the card
- cotton balls
- tongue depressor
- roving or yarn
- hole punch
- scissors
- tape
- glue
- crayons, marking pens, or colored pencils

In Like a Lion, Out Like a Lamb

STEPS TO FOLLOW

1. Color and cut out the patterns.

2. Fringe the outside edge of the yellow plate. Glue the lion's head in the center.

3. Glue the lamb's head in the center of the white plate. Add the ears and cotton balls.

4. Glue the 2 cards to the yellow construction paper.

5. Punch a hole in the edge of the white plate and the corner of the yellow paper. Insert the roving through both. Tie it off in a knot.

6. Tape the tongue depressor to the back of the yellow plate. Glue the back of the white plate to the back of the yellow plate. Allow the glue to dry.

In like a lion, Out like a lamb.

Lamb

March

In like a lion, Out like a lamb.

Lamb's Ears
(black–Cut 2)

Lion

Just like a spring storm, this project is dramatic. Use it as a lead-in to a writing activity about stormy days.

Stormy Weather

MATERIALS

- 9" x 12" (23 x 30.5 cm) light blue construction paper for the background

- 2" x 18" (5 x 45.5 cm) black construction paper for the buildings

- 4" x 6" (10 x 15 cm) white and dark blue construction paper for the clouds

- 2" x 12" (5 x 30.5 cm) yellow construction paper for the lightning and window color

- 9 ½" x 12 ½" (24 x 31.5 cm) black construction paper for the frame

- blue tempera paint

- toothbrush

- glitter

- hole punch

- scissors

- glue

STEPS TO FOLLOW

1. Cut the black strip of paper into sections and lay it on the light blue paper to establish the skyline of the city.

2. Punch holes in the black pieces to represent windows. Cut pieces of yellow paper to glue behind the black to illuminate some of the windows.

3. Glue the buildings in place.

4. Sketch a cloud shape on the white paper. Hold the white and the dark blue paper together as you cut out the drawn shape. Glue them both in place, allowing the blue to slip below the white.

5. Use the toothbrush dipped in blue tempera to "flick" splatters all over the paper. Hint: This process requires close supervision. Allow the paint to dry.

6. Sketch a streak of lightning on the yellow paper. Cut it out. Apply a strip of glue down the center and dribble glitter onto it. Press lightly and then shake off the excess. Allow to dry.

7. Glue the lightning in the sky.

8. Frame the picture by gluing it to the black paper.

A Colorful Windsock

Join students in a spring parade around the playground, letting the wind blow your colorful windsocks about.

STEPS TO FOLLOW

1. Sketch a wavy line on the yellow paper strip as shown. Cut on the line.

2. Glue the yellow strip to the top edge of the orange paper.

3. Cut circles of varying sizes from the yellow, blue, and pink paper. Glue them in a random fashion onto the orange paper.

4. Flip over the orange paper. Glue the tissue strips evenly spaced along the bottom edge.

5. Roll the orange paper into a cylinder and staple. Secure the rest of the opening with tape.

6. Punch two holes opposite each other on the yellow perimeter. Tie a piece of string through each hole. Tie the opposite ends together.

7. Tape the ends of the strings to the tongue depressor, which acts as a handle.

MATERIALS

- 12" x 15" (30.5 x 38 cm) orange construction paper for the base

- 4" x 18" (10 x 45.5 cm) yellow construction paper for the cuff

- 6" (15 cm) squares of pink, yellow, and blue construction paper for decoration

- 10—1" x 9" (2.5 x 23 cm) strips of tissue paper

- tongue depressor

- string

- tape

- stapler

- hole punch

- scissors

- glue

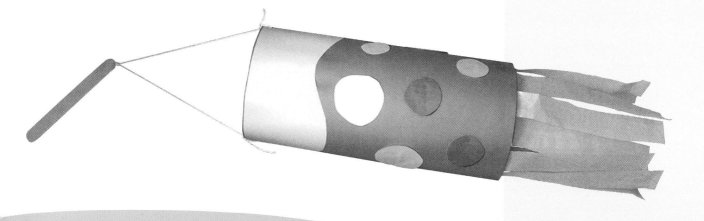

Art for All Seasons • EMC 2001 • ©2004 by Evan-Moor Corp.

Students can make their flowers "grow" by reaching inside the folder and pushing up the tongue depressor.

MATERIALS

- pattern on the following page, reproduced for each student
- 3" (7.5 cm) square of blue construction paper for the flower
- 1 ½" (4 cm) square of yellow construction paper for the flower center
- 1 ½" x 2" (4 x 5 cm) green construction paper for the leaves
- 1" (2.5 cm) square of red construction paper for the ladybug
- 6" x 8 ½" (15 x 21.5 cm) green construction paper for the frame
- craft knife
- crayons, marking pens, or colored pencils
- tongue depressor
- scissors
- glue
- tape (optional)

Watch My Flower Grow

STEPS TO FOLLOW

1. Color the pattern. Add a colorful background.
2. Cut the slit as marked. You may reinforce the slit edges with tape in case of heavy use.
3. Fold the paper in half.
4. Cut circles from the blue and yellow squares. Glue the yellow circle in the center of the blue. Fringe around the outside edge of the blue circle.
5. Cut 2 leaves from the green paper.
6. Use the red square to make a ladybug. Glue the ladybug to the flower.
7. Glue the flower and the leaves to the end of the tongue depressor. Slip the other end of the tongue depressor through the slit.
8. Glue the backside of the pattern to the green frame and watch the flower grow.

slit

fold

Hang these bright and colorful banners around the school as a welcome to spring.

Tissue Paper Banner

MATERIALS

- pattern and templates on the following page
- 6—5" (12.5 cm) squares of tissue in bright colors for the flowers
- 6—2" (5 cm) squares of tissue in the same colors for the flower centers
- 2—10" x 18" (25.5 x 45.5 cm) strips of clear contact paper or laminate
- 6" x 10" (15 x 25.5 cm) orange construction paper for the headpiece
- roving or yarn
- 1" x 12" (2.5 x 30.5 cm) strips of cellophane
- hole punch
- scissors
- double-stick tape
- glue

STEPS TO FOLLOW

1. Trace around the templates for the flower shape on one of the larger tissue paper squares. Place all the larger tissue squares together and cut out the shape.

2. Trace the flower center on one of the smaller squares of tissue. Place them all together and cut them out.

3. Pull the backing off one of the contact strips. Lay it sticky side up on the table. Lay the flowers and their centers overlapping slightly on the contact paper.

4. Position the cellophane strips along the bottom of the banner.

5. Pull the backing off the second contact strip. Now have a friend help lay the contact paper over the top of the tissue flowers. Press to seal the two pieces of contact paper together.

6. Fold the orange construction paper in half. Glue the Hooray! It's Spring! sign to one side.

7. Use double-stick tape to secure the folded construction paper to the top of the banner.

8. Punch two holes in the orange headpiece. Tie roving through each one to create the hanger strip.

Hooray! It's Spring!

Tissue Paper Banner
PATTERN AND TEMPLATES

Sign Pattern

Flower

Flower Center

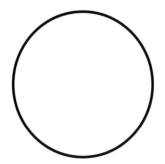

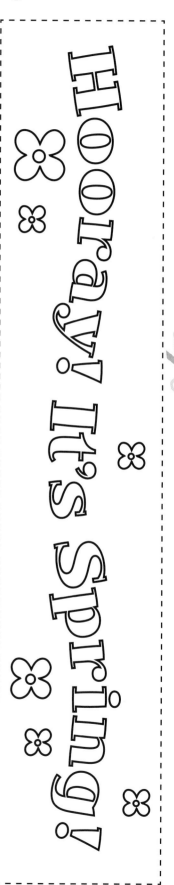

Make a bunch of these little fellows, positioning heads, beaks, and wings differently. Display them in a line on the windowsill or in your classroom library along with a copy of *Make Way for Ducklings.*

Delightful Ducklings

MATERIALS

- templates on the following page
- 6" x 9" (15 x 23 cm) yellow construction paper for the body, head, and wings
- 3 ½" (9 cm) square of orange construction paper for the feet and beak
- scissors
- glue
- crayons, marking pens, or colored pencils

STEPS TO FOLLOW

1. Trace around the templates on the yellow and orange paper. Cut on the lines.
2. Fold the circles for the body and the wings in half.
3. Cut the wing circle on the fold line so there are now 2 half circles.
4. Fold the beak piece in half. Glue it to the head. Add eyes with crayons, marking pens, or colored pencils.
5. Glue the head and wings to the body. Experiment with positions to create different effects.
6. Fold the feet piece in half and trim at an angle.
7. Glue the body to the feet.

Body (yellow)

Head/Wings (yellow–Cut 2)

Beak (orange)

Feet (orange)

Body (yellow)

Head/Wings (yellow–Cut 2)

Beak (orange)

Feet (orange)

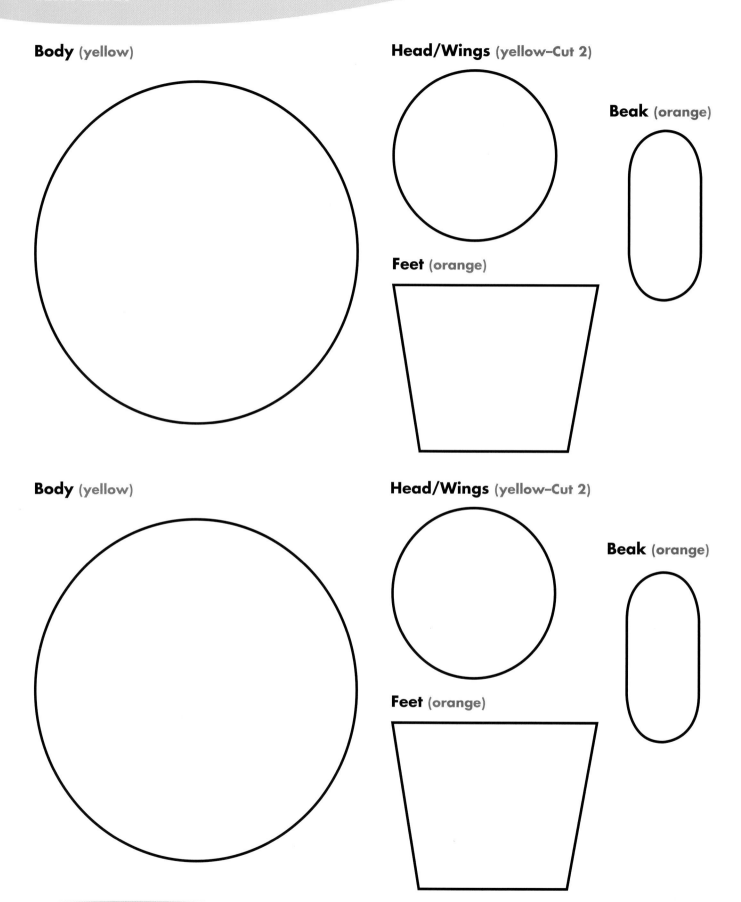

Part of the fun of making this jolly leprechaun is the combination of printing techniques and paper construction.

MATERIALS

- templates on the following page
- 6" x 9" (15 x 23 cm) green construction paper for the torso, legs, arms, and hat
- 3" x 4" (7.5 x 10 cm) pink construction paper for the head and hands
- 3" x 4" (7.5 x 10 cm) black construction paper for the feet and vest
- 10" x 12" (25.5 x 30.5 cm) white paper for the background
- 10 ½" x 12 ½" (26.5 x 32 cm) black construction paper for the frame
- carrot slices
- yellow, green, and orange tempera paint
- shallow dishes
- pencil with a new eraser
- scissors
- glue
- crayons, marking pens, or colored pencils

The Mischievous Leprechaun

STEPS TO FOLLOW

1. Trace around and cut out the patterns from the green, pink, and black paper.

2. Lay out all the parts on the white paper. Experiment with creating the leprechaun in different positions. The arms and legs can bend if you cut a slit as marked on the template.

3. Glue all the parts together. Then glue them to the white construction paper background.

4. Use the tempera paint to add the background:
   Orange paint printed with a pencil eraser creates the hair.
   Yellow paint printed with a pencil eraser creates gold coins.
   Green paint printed with carrot slices creates shamrocks.

5. Add details to the face, clothes, and background with crayons, marking pens, or colored pencils.

6. Glue the white paper to the black paper frame.

Torso (green)

Arm (green–Cut 2)

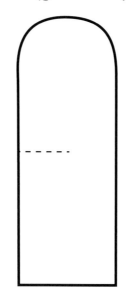

Leg (green–Cut 2)

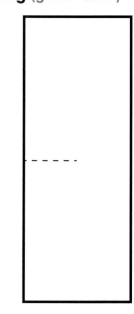

Hat (green)

Head (pink)

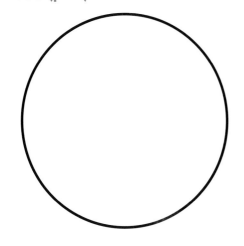

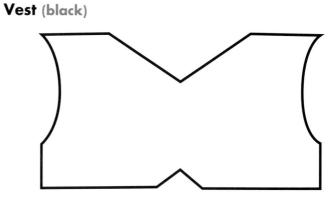

Vest (black)

Hand (pink–Cut 2)

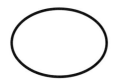

Feet (black—Cut 2)

This unfolding, pop-up card is a dramatic way to say, "Happy Saint Patrick's Day."

MATERIALS

- patterns on the following page, reproduced for each student
- 14" (35.5 cm) square of green construction paper for the shamrock covering
- 6" x 12" (15 x 30.5 cm) blue construction paper for the pop-up card
- crayons, marking pens, or colored pencils
- scissors
- glue
- ruler

At the End of the Rainbow Card

STEPS TO FOLLOW

1. Fold the green paper as shown.

2. Trim off the outside corners. Open the paper to discover that you have created a shamrock.

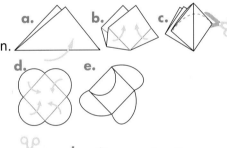

3. Fold the blue paper in half. Cut two slits as shown.

4. Fold the cut tab to the front. Then turn it over and fold it to the back. Open the card and pull the tab to the inside.

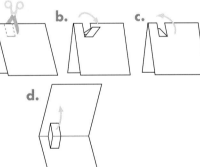

5. Color and cut out the patterns. Write a greeting for the card on the lined form.

6. Glue the rainbow to the front of the blue card.

7. Glue the pot of gold to the inside pop-up tab. Glue the greeting form below the pot of gold.

8. Glue the blue paper to the center of the shamrock. Fold the leaves of the shamrock around the blue paper.

9. Glue on the Happy Saint Patrick's Day sticker to keep the card closed.

Front

Sticker

Happy
Saint
Patrick's
Day

At the End
of the
Rainbow!

Paste on pop-up tab.

A Pot of
Gold!

Greeting Form

Spring Surprises

MATERIALS

- 5" x 18" (12.5 x 45.5 cm) green construction paper for the grass
- ¾" x 6" (2 x 15 cm) yellow construction paper strip for the worm
- several 2" (5 cm) squares of white copy paper for the wildflowers
- paper scraps in assorted colors for the flower centers and leaves
- pencil
- scissors
- glue
- crayons, marking pens, or colored pencils

STEPS TO FOLLOW

1. Fold the green paper into quarters as shown. Sketch a zigzag line on one open end. Cut on that line.

   a.   b.   c.

2. Open the green accordion-folded paper. It looks like a grassy strip. Plan how many flowers you will add. Each flower is made by rolling the paper into a cone over your finger and gluing it.

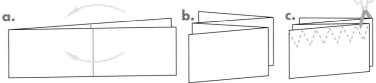

3. The center of each flower is made by rolling a narrow strip of construction paper around a pencil and then gluing one end inside the flower. Leaves may also be cut from scraps.

4. Glue the completed flowers and leaves to the grassy strip.

5. Add stems with crayons, marking pens, or colored pencils.

6. Round the corners on the yellow strip for the worm. Add details with colored pencils. Stand up the accordion-folded project and wind the worm through the blades of grass.

A Chain of Eggs Card

1. Color the patterns using the side of a crayon.

2. Cut out the patterns. Fold on the fold line and cut the inner line.

3. Lift the flap of the blue egg and slip it through the hole of the red egg. Then lift the flap of the yellow egg and slip it through the hole of the blue egg. Now you have a chain of eggs.

4. Lay the eggs on the blue paper. Punch 2 holes as indicated on the egg pattern. Insert the roving and tie a bow.

5. Glue the grass and Happy Easter greeting onto the bottom of the blue paper.

This project makes a cute Easter card. Students may also enjoy connecting their chains with others in the classroom to create a decorative border for a bulletin board.

MATERIALS

- patterns on the following page, reproduced for each student

- 4 ½" x 9 ½" (11 x 24 cm) blue construction paper for the background

- yellow roving or yarn

- crayons

- scissors

- hole punch

- glue

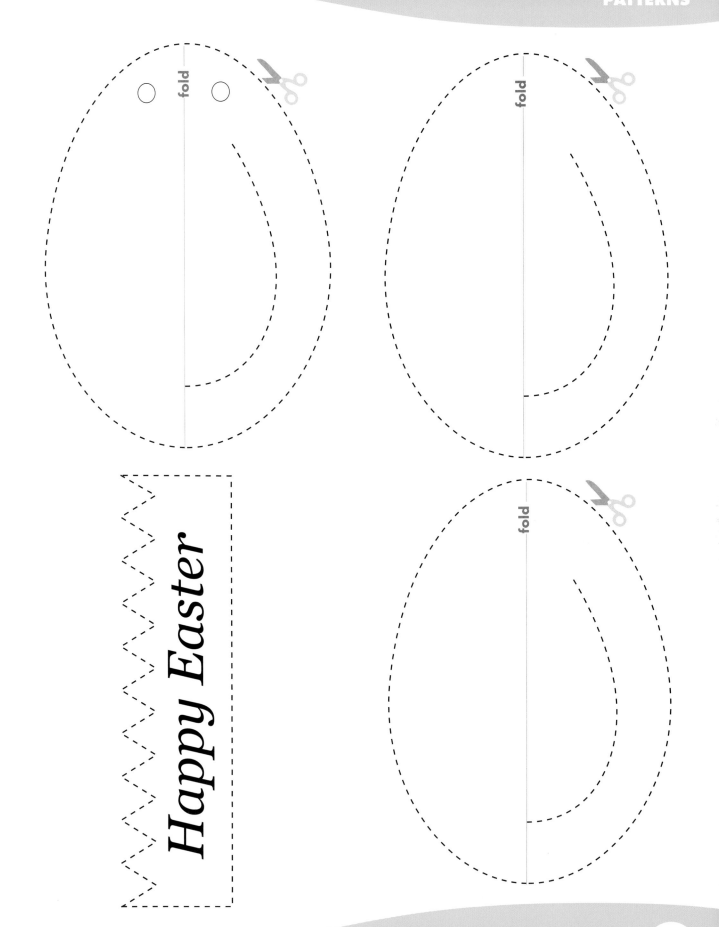

Happy Easter

A Basket Full of Fun

Paper weaving lends visual interest to this charming project.

STEPS TO FOLLOW

1. Use the craft knife to make 10—5" (12.5 cm) vertical slits in the blue paper as shown.

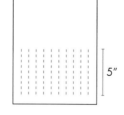
5"

2. Weave the 7 orange strips into the slits. Push the strips to the bottom and glue the edges. There will be room to add more strips, but it is only there to make it easier to do the weaving. That area will be covered up by the eggs and grass.

3. Fold the orange paper for the handle. Place the template on the fold and trace around it. Cut on the lines and glue in place on the basket.

4. Cut out the grass, eggs, and chicks using the templates as a guide. Lay them on the blue paper.

5. Glue all the parts in place. Notice that the chicks need to be under the eggs, and the eggs go under the grass.

6. Use the orange paper scraps for beaks and a black marking pen to add eyes to the chicks.

7. Accordion-fold the pink tissue paper. Twist it in the middle and glue it to the handle of the basket.

8. Glue the blue paper to the yellow paper frame.

MATERIALS

- templates on the following page
- 9" x 12" (23 x 30.5 cm) dark blue construction paper for the background
- 9 ½" x 12 ½" (24 x 32 cm) yellow construction paper for the frame
- 7—½" x 6 ½" (1.25 x 16.5 cm) orange construction paper for the basket
- 6" x 7" (16.5 x 18 cm) orange construction paper for the handle
- 1" x 7" (2.5 x 18 cm) green construction paper for the grass
- 4—3" (7.5 cm) squares of pink and purple construction paper for the eggs (2 each)
- 4—1 ½" (4 cm) squares of yellow construction paper for the chicks
- orange scraps for beaks
- 4" x 6" (10 x 15 cm) pink tissue paper for the bow
- craft knife
- black marking pen
- glue
- scissors

Art for All Seasons • EMC 2001 • ©2004 by Evan-Moor Corp.

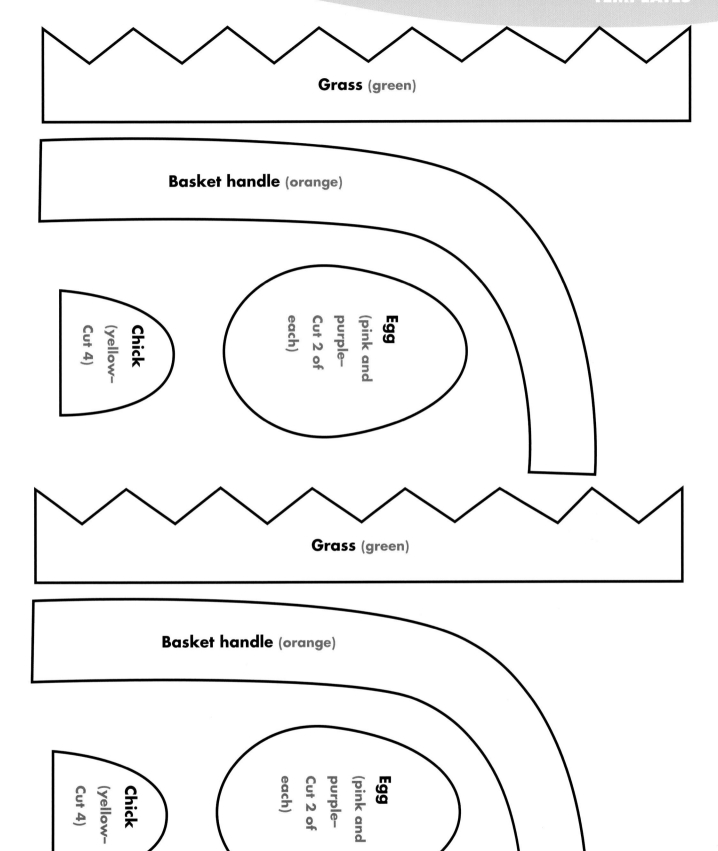

Grass (green)

Basket handle (orange)

Chick (yellow– Cut 4)

Egg (pink and purple– Cut 2 of each)

Grass (green)

Basket handle (orange)

Chick (yellow– Cut 4)

Egg (pink and purple– Cut 2 of each)

Watch It Hatch

The 3-D aspects turn this simple project into something really special.

MATERIALS

- patterns on the following page, reproduced for each student

  Hint: These patterns may be used as templates if you want to create the project with construction paper instead of copy paper.

- 5" x 7" (12.5 x 18 cm) light blue construction paper for the backing

- 5 ½" x 9 ½" (14 x 24 cm) green construction paper for the frame and grass

- scissors

- pencil

- glue

- black marking pen

STEPS TO FOLLOW

1. Color and cut out the patterns. Cut the inside lines on the egg. Curl each section back using a pencil.

2. Glue the egg to the blue paper.

3. Follow the folding directions for the parts of the chick. Add the orange beak and black eyes. Glue the head to the neck. Glue the other end of the neck inside the egg opening. Glue the 2 wings below the head.

4. Cut a zigzag line on the bottom end of the green paper.

5. Glue the blue paper to the green paper. Fold up the zigzagged bottom over the blue paper.

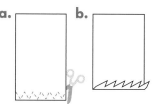

Egg (white)

Head (yellow)

Neck (yellow)

fold

fold

Wings (yellow)

Beak (orange)

fold

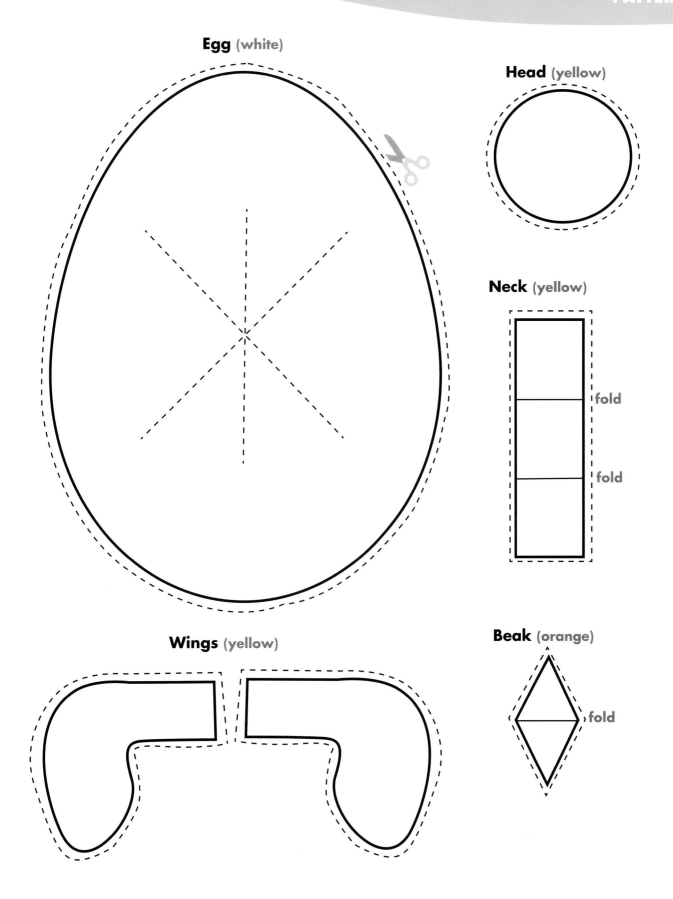

Bunny Headband

MATERIALS

- a brown lunch bag
- 1" (2.5 cm) squares of pink, white, and black construction paper for the nose and eyes
- scraps of black construction paper for the whiskers
- crayons, marking pens, or colored pencils
- scissors
- glue
- stapler
- pencil

STEPS TO FOLLOW

1. Cut the brown lunch bag as shown.

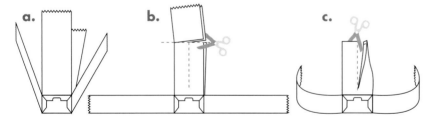

2. Cut down the center panel for the ears. Trim off excess on the ears as shown.

3. Color a pink stripe down the center of each ear.

4. Create the bunny's face by cutting the pink, white, and black paper to create the eyes and nose. Cut and curl the whiskers and add a little mouth.

5. Pinch closed and staple the top of each ear.

6. Fit the headband to each child's head, remove, and staple in place.

This box becomes a memorable Easter basket to share with family and friends. It can also become a container to hold classroom centers.

MATERIALS

- templates on the following page
- shoebox
- 9" (23 cm) square of brown construction paper for the ears and paws
- 12" (30.5 cm) square of pink construction paper for the trim on the ears, paws, and tail
- 2" (5 cm) squares of pink, white, and black construction paper for the nose and eyes
- scraps of black construction paper for the whiskers
- 2" x 8" (5 x 20 cm) orange construction paper for the carrot
- scraps of green construction paper for the carrot stem
- brown tempera paint
- small sponges
- 4 or 5 cotton balls
- basket grass
- black marking pen
- pinking shears

A Bunny Box

STEPS TO FOLLOW

1. Use the sponges dipped in the brown tempera to paint the outside of the shoebox. Allow it to dry thoroughly.

2. Use the templates to guide in cutting out the ears and paws from the brown construction paper. Cut the inner ears, under paws, and tail from pink construction paper.

3. Glue the cotton balls to the tail.

4. Cut the eye and nose pieces from the white, black, and pink construction paper. Cut the whiskers from scraps of black.

5. Glue all the parts to the box. Add a bunny mouth with a black marking pen.

6. Cut a carrot and add a stem. Tuck it in the bunny's paws.

7. Fill the shoebox with basket grass.

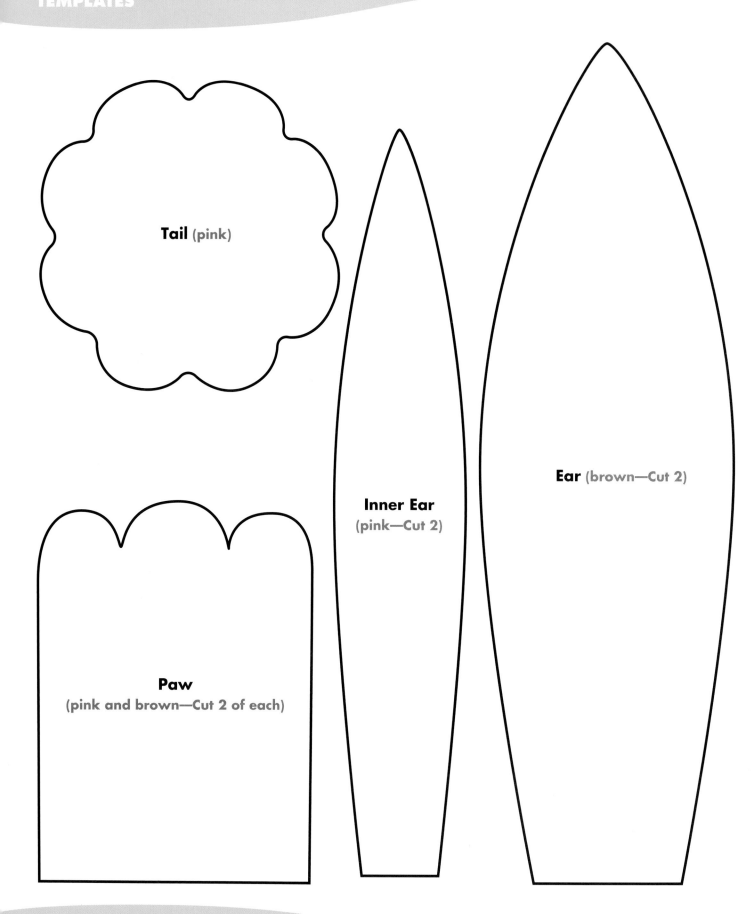

Tail (pink)

Inner Ear
(pink—Cut 2)

Ear (brown—Cut 2)

Paw
(pink and brown—Cut 2 of each)

This bunny is fun and easy to make. It will make a terrific cover for creative stories about rabbits.

Bunny in the Grass

MATERIALS

- patterns on the following page, reproduced for each student
- 9" x 11 ½" (23 x 29 cm) light blue construction paper for the background
- 3" x 11 ½" (7.5 x 29 cm) green construction paper for the grass
- 9 ½" x 12" (24 x 30.5 cm) pink construction paper for the frame
- crayons, marking pens, or colored pencils
- cotton ball
- scissors
- glue

STEPS TO FOLLOW

1. Color and cut out the patterns.
2. Fringe a long side of the green paper.
3. Glue the green paper to the blue background paper.
4. Arrange the pattern pieces to create the bunny. Slip the pieces under the green grass fringe. Glue the parts in place. Leave the tips of the ears free so they can bend forward to add a 3-dimensional quality.
5. Add the cotton-ball tail.
6. Glue the blue background paper to the pink paper frame.

Head

Body

Ears

Students can recycle egg cartons and make a wonderful centerpiece to take home for Easter at the same time.

Easter Centerpiece

MATERIALS

- patterns on the following page, reproduced for each student
- bottom half of an egg carton
- basket grass
- pipe cleaners
- crayons, marking pens, or colored pencils
- scissors
- glue
- tape

STEPS TO FOLLOW

1. Color and cut out the pattern pieces. Students may want to make more than one sheet of patterns.

2. Tape the bee and flowers to varied lengths of pipe cleaner. Make a centrally located hole in the egg carton with the end of the scissors. Insert the pipe cleaners into the hole. Bend the pipe cleaners to fan them out.

3. Glue the bunny, eggs, and bird into the egg carton.

4. Distribute the grass around the items inside the egg carton.

Easter Centerpiece
PATTERNS

Flower

Tulip

Bunny

Chicks

Eggs

Bee

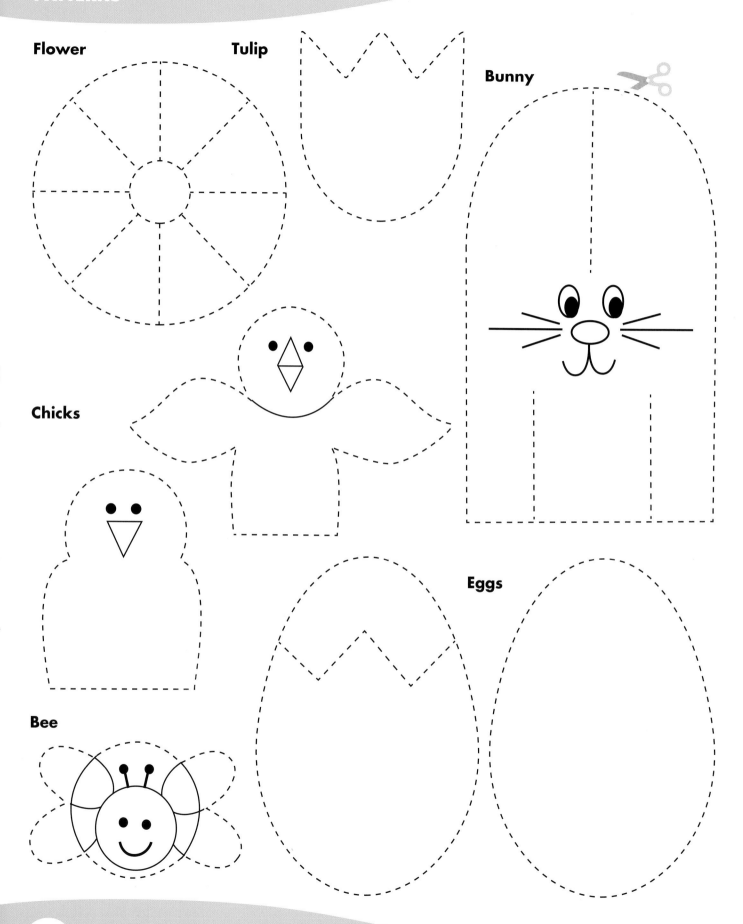

Art for All Seasons • EMC 2001 • ©2004 by Evan-Moor Corp.

Use these bunny chains everywhere. Make a border for your spring bulletin boards. Line them up along the bookcase or windowsill. Use them to motivate student story writing.

MATERIALS

- bunny templates on the following page
- 6" x 18" (15 x 45.5 cm) white construction paper for the chain
- crayons, marking pens, or colored pencils
- scissors
- 4 cotton balls (optional)

A Chain of Bunnies

STEPS TO FOLLOW

1. Fold the white paper as shown.

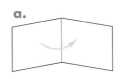

a.   b.   c.

2. Place the template on the folded paper so that the paws and feet are on the folds. Trace and cut out the shape.

3. Open the chain. Use the crayons, marking pens, or colored pencils to make the bunnies' faces and outfits. Students may also want to draw the "rear views" for their bunnies. Just flip the chain over and add those fluffy little cotton-ball tails.

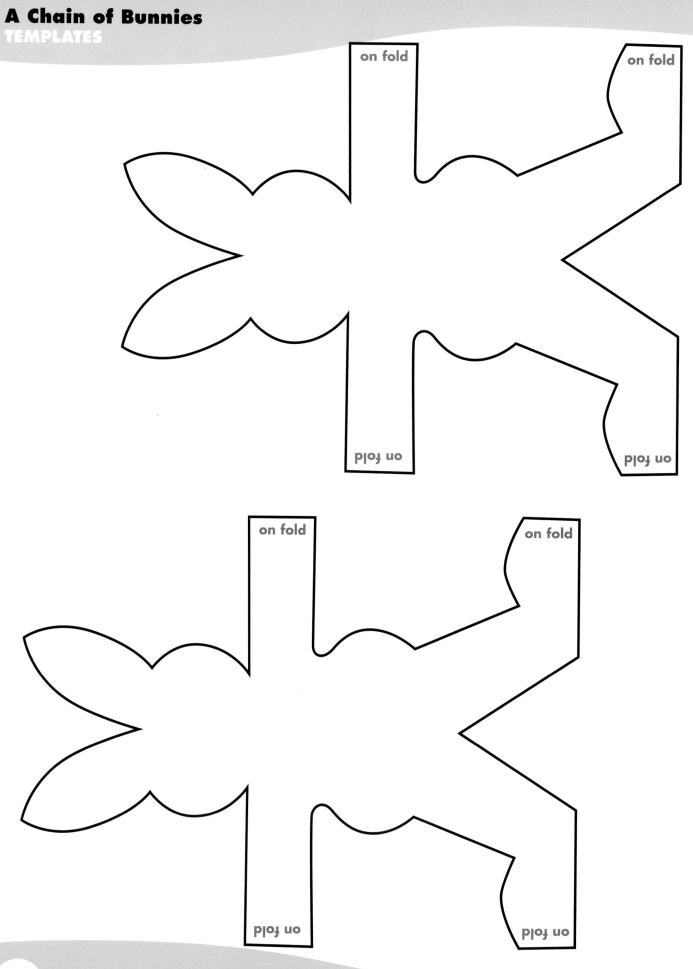

on fold

on fold

on fold

on fold

on fold

on fold

on fold

on fold

Busy Bunnies

Bendable arms and legs allow students to pose their bunnies in a variety of ways. No two projects will be alike.

MATERIALS

- patterns on the following page, reproduced for each student
- 9" x 12" (23 x 30.5 cm) light blue construction paper for the background
- 9½" x 12½" (24 x 32 cm) pink construction paper for the frame
- 2 cotton balls
- crayons, marking pens, or colored pencils
- scissors
- glue

STEPS TO FOLLOW

1. Cut out the pattern pieces. Lay the bunny parts on the blue paper. Arrange them into two bunnies. The fun part is being able to bend the arms and legs to create different positions. Students should experiment with different postures.

2. Glue the parts in place when students are happy with their arrangements.

3. Draw in details on the bunnies with crayons, marking pens, or colored pencils. Also add details to the background.

4. Glue a cotton ball tail to each bunny.

5. Glue the blue paper to the pink frame.

Bunny 1

Bunny 2

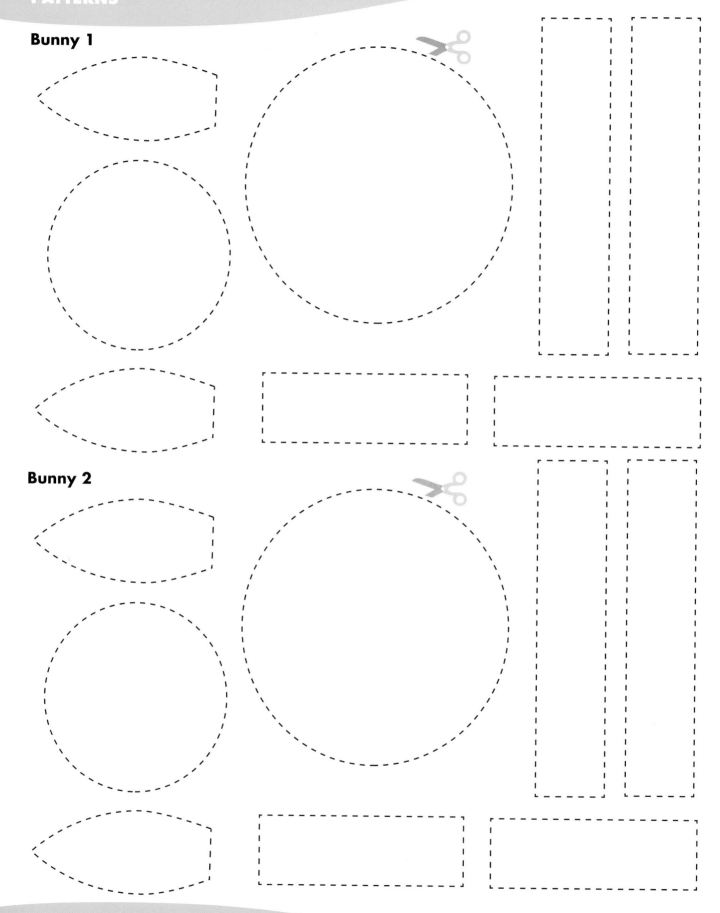

Art for All Seasons • EMC 2001 • ©2004 by Evan-Moor Corp.

The Cross-Legged Bunny

This bunny has his own basket pocket to hold colorful eggs. The eggs in the pocket may have the week's spelling words on them, math facts to practice, or words to use in creative writing.

MATERIALS

- 6" (15 cm) square of white construction paper for the cross-legged body
- 3" (7.5 cm) square of white construction paper for the ears and arms
- 2" (5 cm) squares of colored construction paper for the eggs
- crayons, marking pens, or colored pencils
- scissors
- glue
- stapler

STEPS TO FOLLOW

1. Fold the basic cross-legged body.

a.

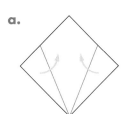

Fold into middle.

b.

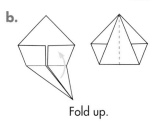

Fold up.

c.

Cut up to the fold. Use crayons, marking pens, or colored pencils to color in the basket. Add facial features.

d.

Cross the bunny's legs and staple. Pull out the basket pieces and staple. Round off the top point and the feet.

2. Cut the ears and arms as shown. Color the inner ears pink. Glue the arms and ears in place.

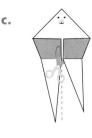

3. Cut egg shapes from the colored squares. Place them in the bunny's pocket. Glue one in his paw.

A Bunny Pop-Up

Friends and family members will be really impressed when students present them with this pop-up card.

MATERIALS

- patterns on the following page, reproduced for each student
- 5 ½" x 8 ½" (14 x 21.5 cm) blue construction paper for the frame
- 5" x 7" (12.5 x 18 cm) yellow construction paper for the background
- 6" x 12 ½" (15 x 32 cm) yellow construction paper for the envelope
- 3" (7.5 cm) square of blue construction paper for the hinges on the envelope
- ruler
- crayons, marking pens, or colored pencils
- scissors
- glue

STEPS TO FOLLOW

1. Color and cut out the patterns. Add facial features to the bunny's head.

2. Follow the folding steps to create the pop-up bunny as shown.

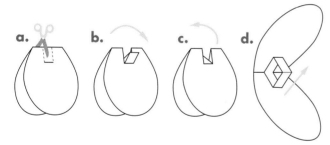

a.   b.   c.   d.

3. Glue the basket to the tab inside the egg. Add the greeting "Happy Easter."

4. Assemble the card parts. Glue the yellow background paper to the blue frame. Lay the bunny head, bow tie, paws, and eggs on the card. Arrange to your liking and glue the parts in place.

5. Fold up 4" (10 cm) of the yellow envelope paper.

6. Fold the small square of blue construction paper in half. Cut on the fold. Round the corners as shown. Fold each blue strip in half. Glue them to the envelope as hinges to hold it closed.

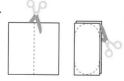

7. Slip the card into the envelope. It's ready to give to a friend or family member.

Art for All Seasons • EMC 2001 • ©2004 by Evan-Moor Corp.

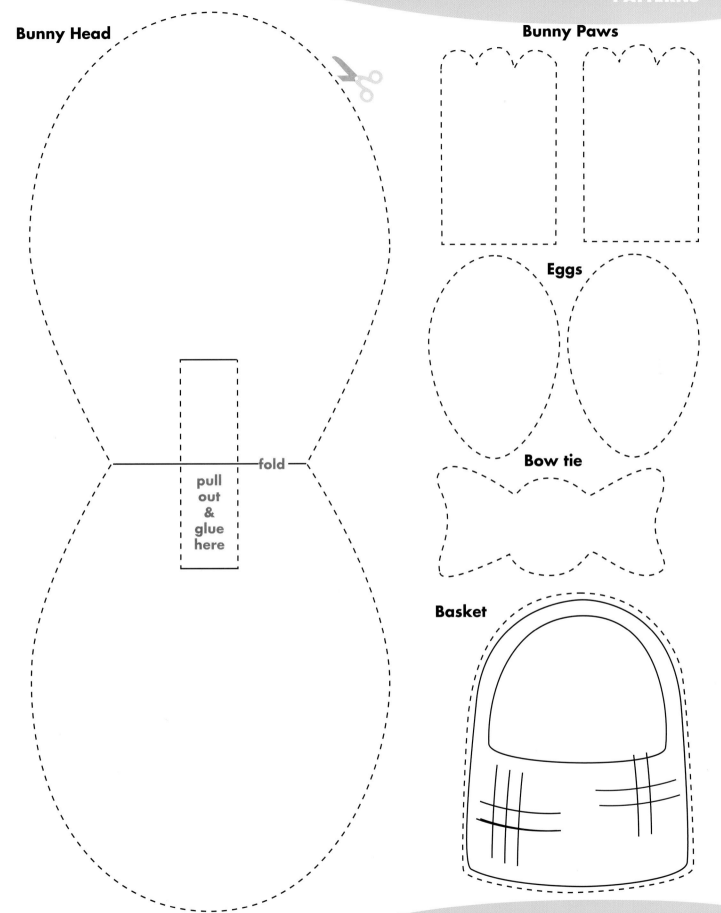

Bunny Head

Bunny Paws

Eggs

pull out & glue here

fold

Bow tie

Basket

A Nifty May Basket

You will love the clever design of this basket. Make them and fill them with flowers to encourage students to participate in the age-old custom of sharing May baskets on the first of May.

STEPS TO FOLLOW

1. Fold the pink square paper into quarters as shown. Open it and mark an X in the center. You will print on this side.

2. Dip the petal-shaped sponge in puddles of the magenta tempera and print one flower in each quarter of the pink paper. Let them dry.

3. Use the pencil eraser to print yellow centers in the flowers. Let them dry.

4. Lay the pink paper flower-side down. Notice that one fold is raised up from corner to corner. Pinch that fold together at one end and pull the fold up to the center. Pinch and pull the opposite corner to the center.

5. Use the hole punch to make lacy dots around the top edge of the basket sections.

6. Punch holes in the handle, too. Continue to decorate the handle by doing pencil-eraser printing with the magenta and yellow tempera.

7. Bend and staple the two ends of the handle to the center of the basket.

8. Cut flowers, centers, and leaves from the small squares of construction paper. Glue them on each side of the handle.

9. Fill the basket with flowers or notes of hello, and surprise a friend.

a.

b.

Put a finger in the center where the two folds cross.

a.

pinch and pull up

pinch and pull up

b.

Cross them over and staple.

MATERIALS

- 12" (30.5 cm) square of pink construction paper for the basket

- 2" x 12" (5 x 30.5 cm) strip of pink construction paper for the handle

- 2" (5 cm) squares of yellow, magenta, and green construction paper for the flowers and leaves

- small petal-shaped sponge

- magenta and yellow tempera paint

- shallow dishes

- pencil with a new eraser

- hole punch

- stapler

- scissors

- glue

A Jumping Frog

Students will enjoy hearing about the annual Calaveras County Jumping Frog Contest in Angel's Camp, California. This project is worth doing. It also makes a fine addition to a bulletin board to accompany a theme unit on rainforests.

MATERIALS

- 4" x 9" (10 x 23 cm) colored copy paper for the frog's body

  Hint: Copy paper is the ideal weight for this project, but construction paper may also be used.

- 2—¾" x 1" (2 x 2.5 cm) pieces of white construction paper for the eyes

- red construction paper scrap for the tongue

- pencil with a new eraser

- tempera paint in assorted colors

- black marking pen

- scissors

- glue

STEPS TO FOLLOW

1. Fold the copy paper as shown to make the basic frog body.

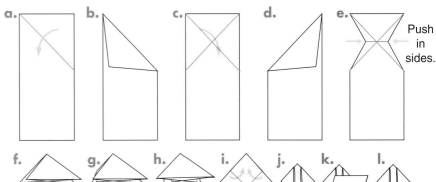

Push in sides.

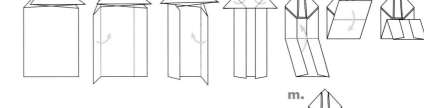

2. Unfold the legs and cut up the center to the second fold for the legs.

3. Round 2 corners on the pieces of white construction paper for the eyes. Add eyeballs with the black marking pen. Fold down a flap on the other end. Glue the folded flap to the frog.

4. Add 2 nostrils with black marking pen.

5. Cut a thin strip of red construction paper for the tongue. Curl the tip with the pencil. Glue it in place.

6. Add spots to the frog's back by using the pencil eraser and tempera in a contrasting color.

7. Stroke the frog's back and watch it jump!

Mom's Wish Express

STEPS TO FOLLOW

1. Fold the blue construction paper accordion style as shown.

a. 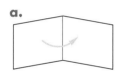 b.   c.

2. Draw tracks for the train along the bottom of the blue paper.

3. Color and cut out the patterns.

4. Complete the 3 Wishes for Mom writing forms. Students write on each form a wish they have for their mom on this Mother's Day.

5. Glue the engine in the first segment of the accordion book. Glue a writing form in each of the 3 remaining segments.

6. On each of the train cars, fold down a flap for gluing. Glue them at the top of each of the 3 sections so that the train cars become flaps that cover the wish forms.

7. Round the corners on the black construction paper squares. Glue 2 of these to each train car as wheels.

This accordion-folded card will be something Mom will cherish forever. It is easy to make and will be a surefire winner when it goes home.

MATERIALS

- patterns on the following 2 pages, reproduced for each student
- 4" x 18" (10 x 45.5 cm) blue construction paper for the background
- 6—1" (2.5 cm) squares of black construction paper for the wheels
- crayons, marking pens, or colored pencils
- pencil
- scissors
- glue

Engine

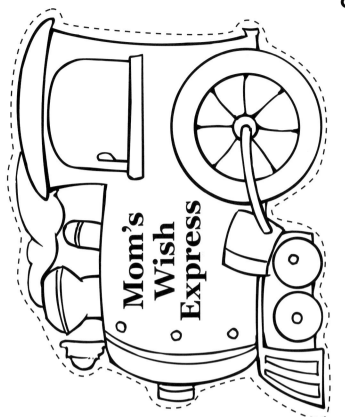

Cattle Car

fold

Coal Car

fold

Caboose

fold

Reproduce enough to provide 3 forms for each student.

Wishes for Mom ...

_____

_____

_____

_____

Wishes for Mom ...

_____

_____

_____

_____

Wishes for Mom ...

_____

_____

_____

_____

Wishes for Mom ...

_____

_____

_____

_____

Wishes for Mom ...

_____

_____

_____

_____

Wishes for Mom ...

_____

_____

_____

_____

Butterfly hover near my mother, Tell her that I dearly love her.

Happy Mother's Day!

Mom

Mother's Day Pop-Up Card

Students will be proud to present this charming card, and Mom will be thrilled to receive it.

MATERIALS

- pattern on the following page, reproduced for each student
- 8" x 11" (20 x 28 cm) blue construction paper for the card
- 3" (7.5 cm) square of yellow construction paper for the clasp
- dark blue stamp pad
- crayons, marking pens, or colored pencils
- scissors
- glue

STEPS TO FOLLOW

1. Color the pattern. Cut out and fold the pop-up card pattern as shown.

   a.

   b.

   Fold forward and back.

   c.

   d.

   Pull pop-up to inside and close.

2. Fold the blue construction paper in half.

3. Use the blue stamp pad and fingers to make little butterflies on the front cover. Add details with crayons, marking pens, or colored pencils.

4. Open the blue paper. Lay the folded pop-up inside, close to the fold. Apply glue. Close the card and press firmly.

   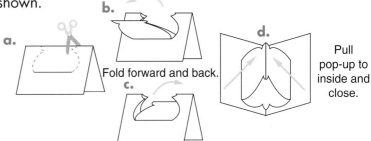

5. Flip the card over and open it. Apply glue to the other side of the pattern. Close the card and press.

6. Round off the corners of the yellow square for the clasp. Fold it in half, apply glue, and wrap around the open side of the card. Write "Mom" on the front. It is ready for delivery!

Tell her that I dearly love her.

Butterfly hover near my mother,

Happy Mother's Day!

This adorable puppy is a nice way to say, "Happy Father's Day."

I'm Glad You're My Dad Puppy

MATERIALS

- patterns and templates on the following page
- 5" x 9" (12.5 x 23 cm) yellow construction paper for the puppy
- 1 ½" (4 cm) square of red construction paper for the puppy's nose
- 3" x 6" (7.5 x 15 cm) brown construction paper for the backing of the bone
- black fine-point marking pen
- scissors
- glue

STEPS TO FOLLOW

1. Cut and fold the yellow construction paper as shown.

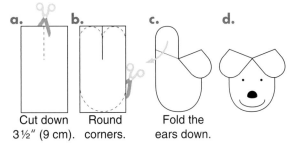

a. Cut down 3½" (9 cm).   b. Round corners.   c. Fold the ears down.   d.

2. Round 2 corners on the red paper for the nose. Glue it in place.

3. Add the eyes, mouth, and whiskers with the black marker.

4. Cut a bone from the brown construction paper using the template as a guide. Cut out a pattern of the smaller bone with the greeting. Glue it to the center of the brown bone.

5. Cut a vertical slit below the nose. Slip the bone into the slit. Glue one end of the bone to the puppy to secure it.

I'm Glad You're My Dad Puppy
TEMPLATES AND PATTERNS

Outer Bone Template (brown)

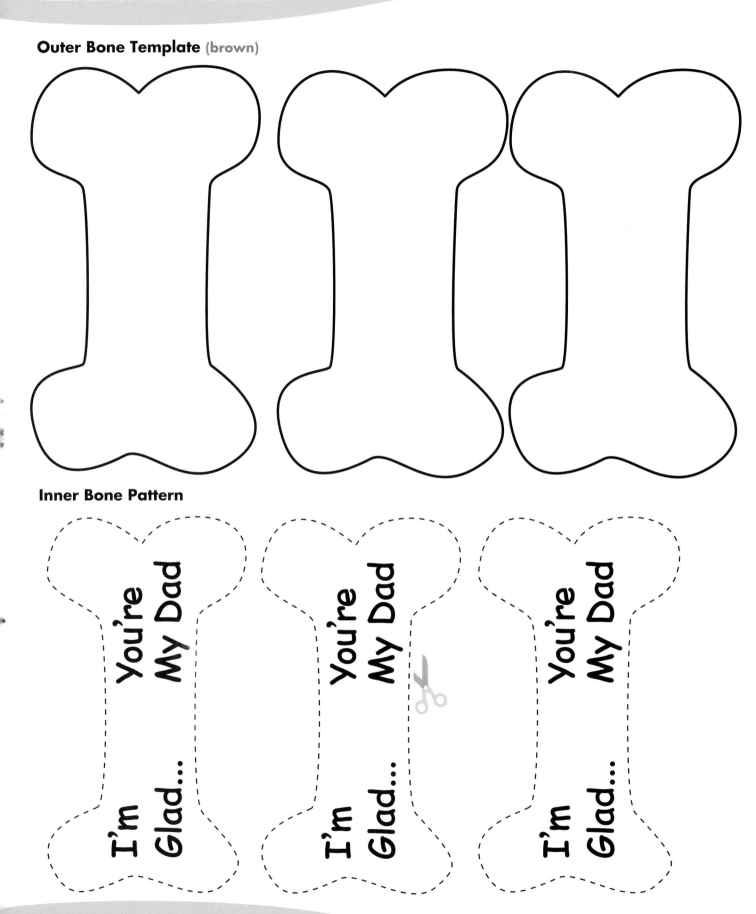

Inner Bone Pattern

You're My Dad I'm Glad...

You're My Dad I'm Glad...

You're My Dad I'm Glad...

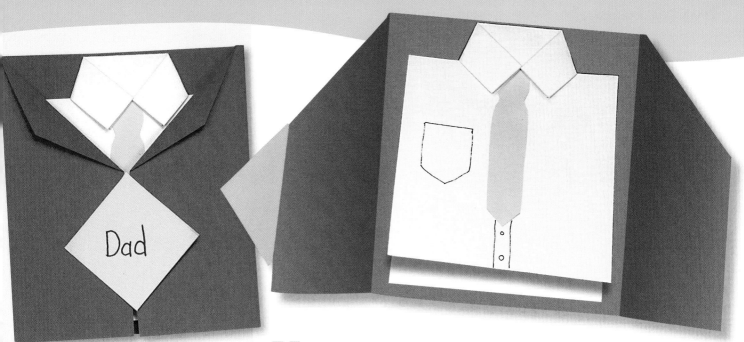

Dad will enjoy this clever little card on his special day.

Happy Father's Day Card

MATERIALS

- pattern and templates on the following page
- 6" x 10 ½" (15 x 26.5 cm) blue construction paper for the cover
- 3" x 4" (7.5 x 10 cm) yellow construction paper for the tie and the cover seal
- scissors
- glue
- black fine-point marking pen

STEPS TO FOLLOW

1. Cut out the shirt pattern. Fold and cut as shown.

a.   **b.**   **c.**

2. Using the template as a guide, cut a tie from the yellow paper. Glue it to the shirt. Add details with the black marking pen.

3. Fold and cut the blue paper as shown.

a.  **b.**   **c.** Fold into center. 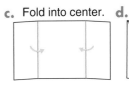 **d.** **e.**

4. Glue the shirt inside the cover.

5. Cut out and glue the seal to the front and address it to Dad.

Happy Father's Day Card
PATTERN & TEMPLATES

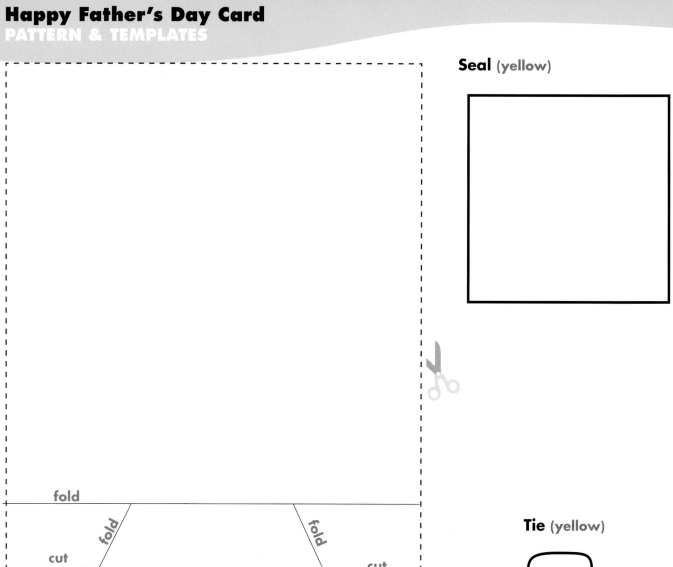

Seal (yellow)

fold

fold

fold

cut

cut

Tie (yellow)

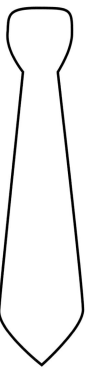

Art for All Seasons • EMC 2001 • ©2004 by Evan-Moor Corp.

Contents

SUMMER

In the Garden

STEPS TO FOLLOW

1. Trace and cut around all the templates on the appropriate colors of paper. Punch holes as indicated.

2. Fold the blue paper for the overalls as shown below.

3. Use crayons, marking pens, or colored pencils to add details to the face and shirt.

4. Glue the head and neck to the overalls.

5. Cut the slit in the hat with a craft knife. Slip the hat over the head. Tape in the back.

6. Cut the brown paper into 4 strips. Glue 2 on each side of the head under the hat for hair.

7. Attach the arms to the overalls with the paper fasteners.

8. Glue the gloves and boots to the little gardener.

9. Glue the trowel onto one glove. Punch holes in the bucket and insert a strip of string. Tie the ends together. Tape the string loop onto the other glove.

10. Add other details with scraps of paper, crayons, marking pens, or colored pencils.

This little gardener can help create a colorful bulletin board for your plant unit.

MATERIALS

- templates on the following 2 pages
- 4" x 9" (10 x 23 cm) blue construction paper for the overalls
- 6" x 8" (15 x 20 cm) yellow construction paper for the hat
- 6" x 12" (15 x 30.5 cm) white construction paper for the face and shirt
- 2" x 10" (5 x 25.5 cm) red construction paper for the gloves and boots
- 2" (5 cm) square of brown construction paper for hair
- 1 ½" x 3 ½" (4 x 9 cm) black construction paper for the trowel
- 2½" x 3" (6 x 7.5 cm) green construction paper for the bucket
- scraps of construction paper for added details
- 2 paper fasteners
- scissors
- glue and tape
- crayons, marking pens, or colored pencils
- hole punch
- craft knife
- string

a. 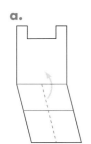   **b.**   **c.**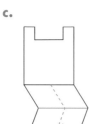

Cut up the center of the overalls for the leg line.

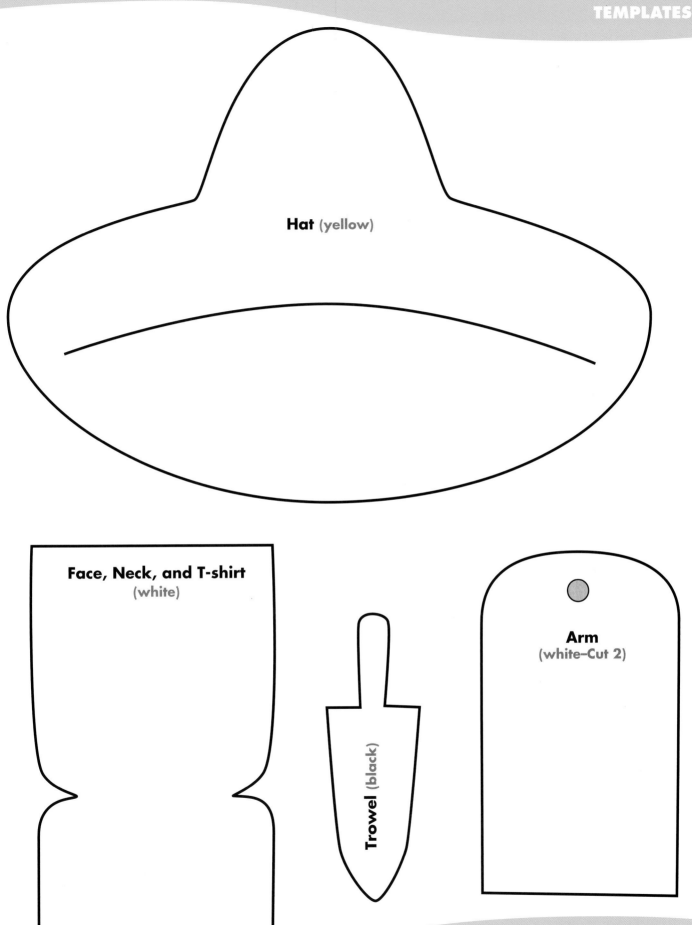

Hat (yellow)

Face, Neck, and T-shirt
(white)

Trowel (black)

Arm
(white–Cut 2)

Garden Glove
(red–Cut 2)

Overalls
(blue)

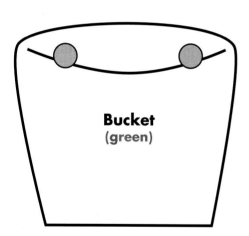

Bucket
(green)

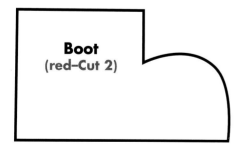

Boot
(red–Cut 2)

After creating this camp-out picture, students will want to write a story describing what is happening.

MATERIALS

- templates and patterns on the following page
- 6" x 7" (15 x 18 cm) brown wrapping paper for the tent
- 9" x 12" (23 x 30.5 cm) dark blue construction paper for the background
- 4" x 5" (10 x 12.5 cm) black construction paper for the tent pieces
- 2½" (6 cm) square of yellow construction paper for the moon
- 2½" x 12" (6 x 30.5 cm) green construction paper strip for the grass
- 9½" x 12½" (24 x 32 cm) yellow construction paper for the frame
- foil star stickers
- scissors
- glue
- crayons, marking pens, or colored pencils

Camping

STEPS TO FOLLOW

1. Cut a zigzag edge on the green strip for grass. Glue it to the bottom of the blue paper.

2. Trace and cut out the tent template. Cut up the center line and fold as indicated.

3. Cut a narrow strip from the black paper for the tent supports.

4. Lay the rest of the black paper and the brown wrapping paper on the background for the tent. Glue in place. Also glue on the tent supports.

5. Using the template as a guide, cut a moon shape from the yellow paper. Glue it in the sky.

6. Color and cut out the campfire and camper patterns. Glue the campfire to one side of the tent.

7. Who is in the tent? Pick one of the patterns and glue it inside the flaps.

8. Finish the picture by placing a few star stickers in the sky.

Camping

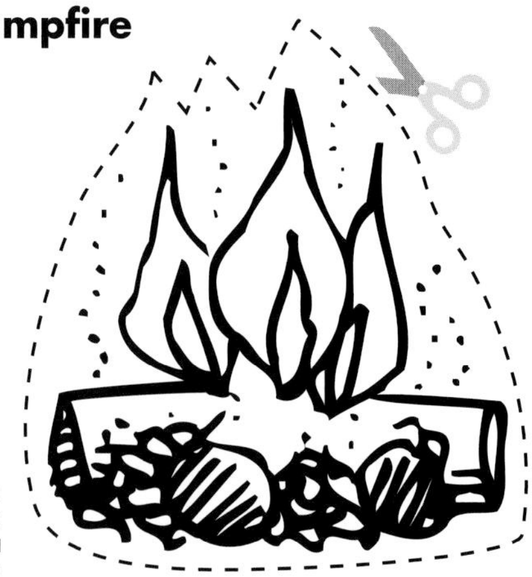

Child—Camper 1

Bear—Camper 2

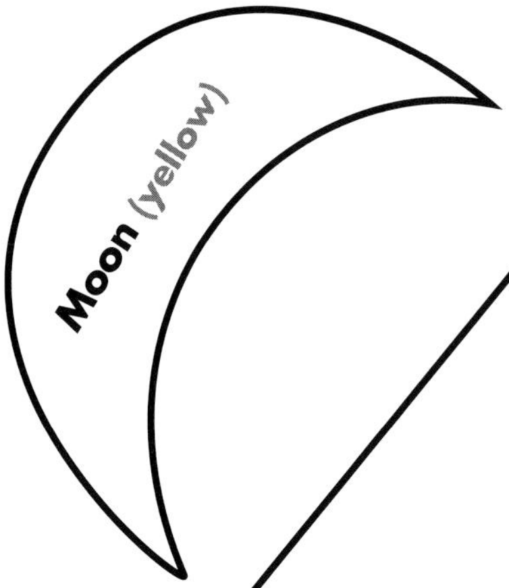

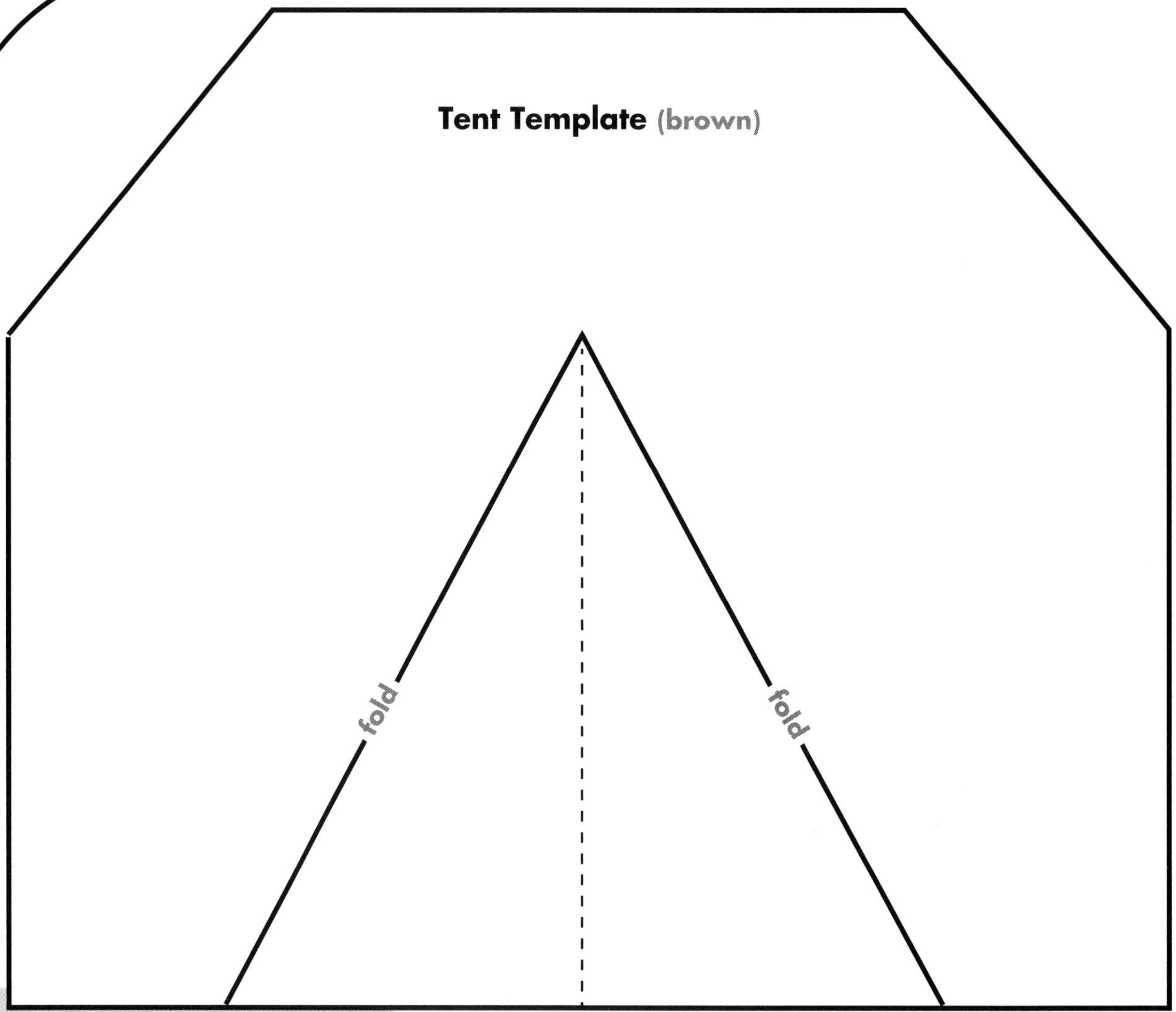

Campfire

Moon (yellow)

Tent Template (brown)

fold

fold

Grasshopper

MATERIALS

- templates on the following page
- 6" x 8" (15 x 20 cm) green construction paper for the grasshopper's body
- 6" (15 cm) square of green construction paper for the grasshopper's legs
- ½" x 4" (1.25 x 10 cm) yellow construction paper for the antennae
- scissors
- glue
- crayons, marking pens, or colored pencils
- pencil

STEPS TO FOLLOW

1. Fold the larger green paper in half.

2. Lay the body template on the fold. Trace around it. Lightly sketch in the parts. Cut it out while it is still folded.

3. Cut the line between the two front legs. Bend the back one toward the rear.

4. Use crayons, marking pens, or colored pencils to outline the details of the body sections, wings, eyes, and mouth.

5. Cut out 2 rear legs using the template as a guide.

6. Fold the two bottom flaps under. Glue them together to create a base for the grasshopper.

7. Glue a leg to each side.

8. Cut down the center of the yellow strip of paper. Fold back one end and glue it inside the head section as an antenna. Curl the end on a pencil. Glue the other one to the other side of the head.

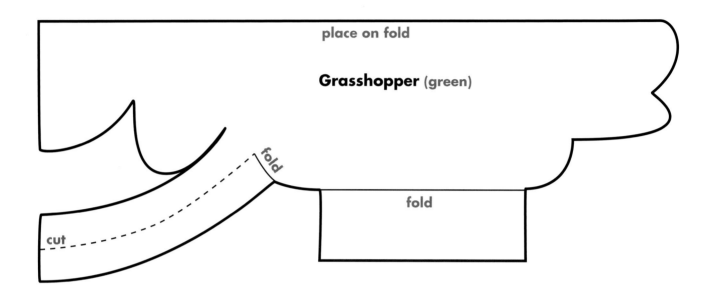

place on fold

Grasshopper (green)

fold

fold

cut

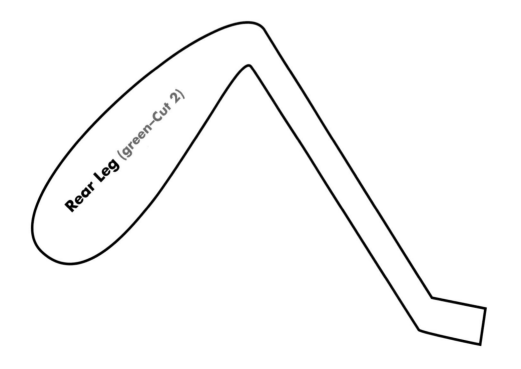

Rear Leg (green–Cut 2)

This bear's gone fishin'. Students can write about his success.

MATERIALS

- templates on the following page
- 11" x 12" (28 x 30.5 cm) brown construction paper for the background
- 3" x 12" (7.5 x 30.5 cm) green construction paper for the treetops
- 2" x 12" (5 x 30.5 cm) blue construction paper for the river
- 7" x 12" (18 x 30.5) black construction paper for the bear's head and body
- 2" x 3" (5 x 7.5 cm) orange construction paper for the fish
- yellow, red, and brown paper scraps for the bear's snout, nose, and eyes
- craft knife
- scissors
- glue
- ruler
- crayons or colored pencils
- hole punch
- black marking pen

Bear in the Woods

STEPS TO FOLLOW

1. Using the craft knife, precut 9 vertical slits in the brown paper as shown. Slits may be wavy and uneven—like tree trunks.

2. Trim one edge of the green paper with scallops to look like the trees in the woods. Glue it to the top of the brown paper.

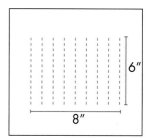

3. Trim one edge of the blue paper with a wavy line to look like water. Glue it to the bottom of the brown paper.

4. Trace around the bear templates on the black paper. Carefully tear out the shapes. Glue the head to the body.

5. Cut out a brown snout and a red nose for the bear. Use the hole punch, yellow paper, and a black marker to make its eyes. Glue in place.

6. Weave the bear's head and body into the slits in the brown paper.

7. Using the template as a guide, cut 3 fish from the orange paper. Add black dots for the eyes. Glue one fish to the bear's snout and the rest in the water.

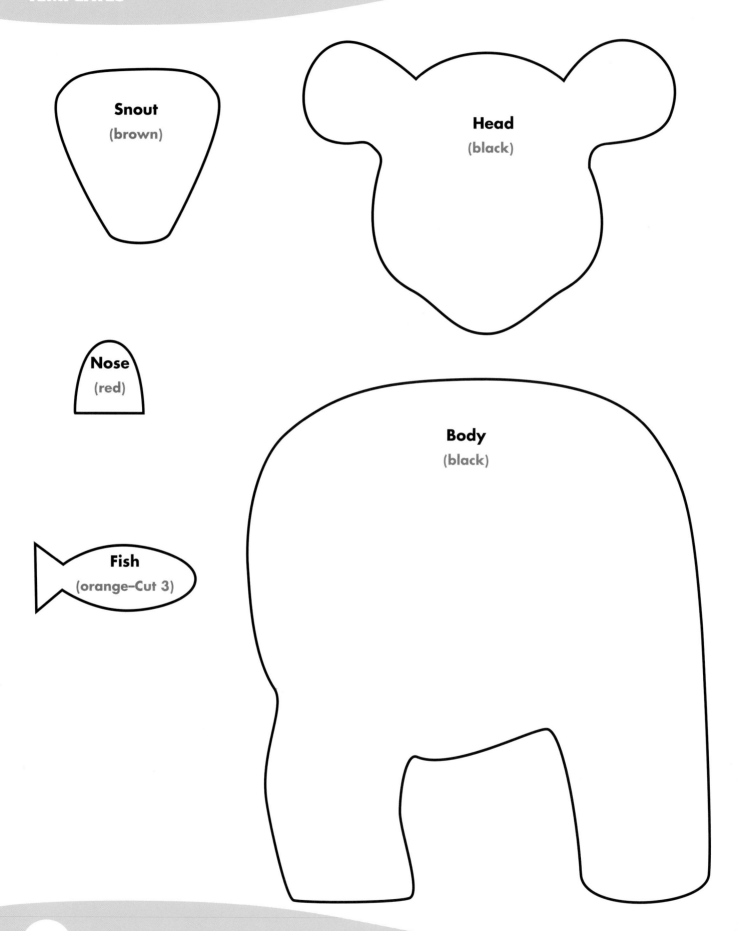

Snout
(brown)

Head
(black)

Nose
(red)

Body
(black)

Fish
(orange–Cut 3)

You can use this project in so many ways. Hang these lovely dragonflies in the classroom, pin them in a cluster on your bulletin board, or let the students enjoy them as miniature kites to fly around the playground.

MATERIALS

- templates on the following page
- 2 ½" x 9" (6 x 23 cm) blue tagboard
- 4—4" x 7" (10 x 18 cm) pieces of pink tissue paper for the wings
- 3" (7.5 cm) square of yellow construction paper for the heart
- 2 black beans
- paper clip
- 18" (45.5 cm) length of clear plastic fishing line
- tongue depressor
- glitter
- scissors
- glue
- tape
- crayons, marking pens, or colored pencils
- stapler

Dragonfly

STEPS TO FOLLOW

1. Trace around the body template onto the blue tagboard. Cut it out and add details with a black marker, colored pencil, or crayon.

2. Glue on the beans for eyes.

3. Tape the paper clip to the back of the face.

4. Make 4 pink tissue paper wings using the template as a guide. Place 2 on each side of the body. Make one pleat in the wings and then staple to the center section.

5. Cut out a yellow heart to glue over where the wings are attached. Add glitter to the heart to give it some sparkle.

6. Tie the fishing line to the paper clip. Tape the other end to the tongue depressor for a handle.

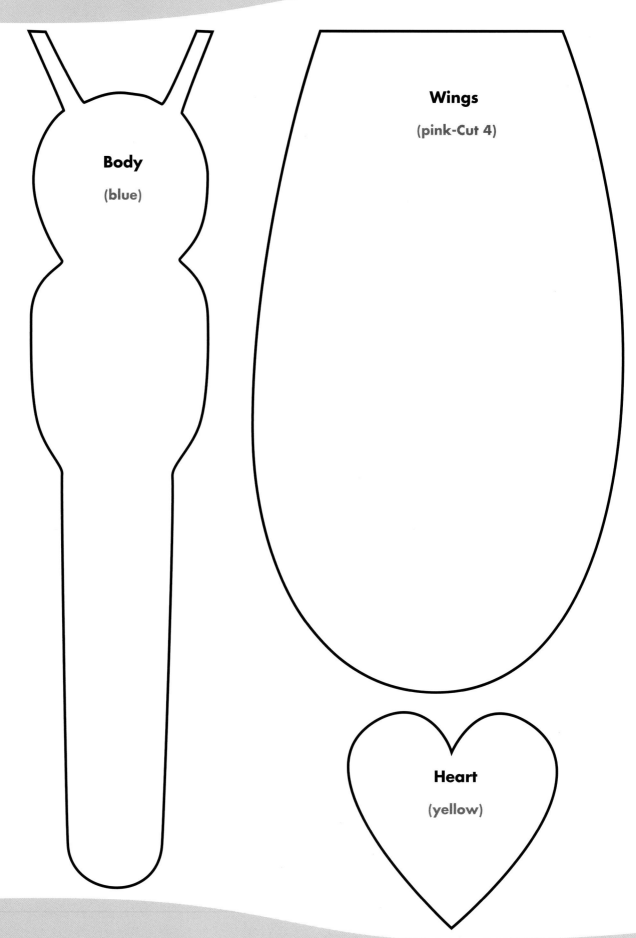

Body

(blue)

Wings

(pink-Cut 4)

Heart

(yellow)

These swimmers are frolicking with their inner tubes between the waves. The lesson may be extended by having students write a sentence or paragraph about their favorite activities at the seaside and then glue it to the back of the blue "waves."

MATERIALS

- templates on the following page
- 5 ½" x 18" (14 x 45.5 cm) white construction paper for the chain
- 12" x 18" (30.5 x 45.5 cm) blue construction paper for the ocean waves
- 2" x 5" (5 x 12.5 cm) red, yellow, blue, and orange construction paper for the inner tubes
- scissors
- glue
- crayons, marking pens, or colored pencils

By the Sea...

STEPS TO FOLLOW

1. Accordion-fold the white paper as shown.

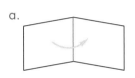

2. Trace the chain template onto the folded paper. Cut on the lines.

3. Use the template to trace the inner tubes on the colorful pieces of construction paper. Cut them out and glue in place on the chain.

4. Color the chain of swimmers, making each one unique.

5. Fold the blue paper as shown.

6. Cut a wave border on the top and bottom of the paper.

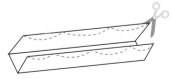

7. Print "By the sea..." along the front wave. Place the chain of swimmers between the two waves.

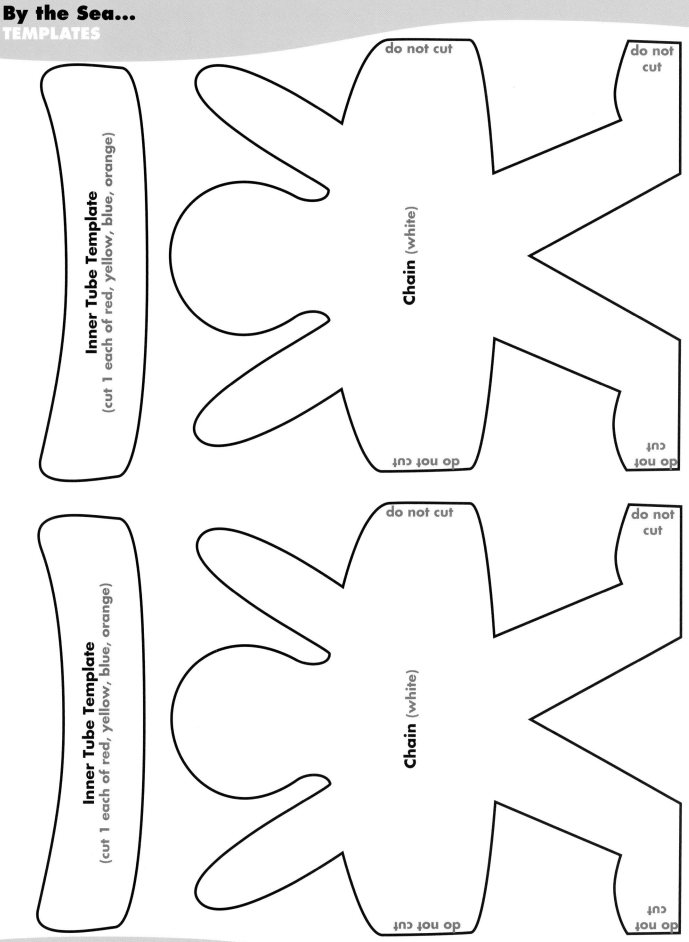

Inner Tube Template
(cut 1 each of red, yellow, blue, orange)

Chain (white)

do not cut

do not cut

do not cut

do not cut

Inner Tube Template
(cut 1 each of red, yellow, blue, orange)

Chain (white)

do not cut

do not cut

do not cut

do not cut

Have students make extra shells to adorn an "under the sea" bulletin board. Use twisted green tissue for an interesting 3-D addition to the board.

Below the Sea

MATERIALS

- templates on the following 2 pages
- 9" x 12" (23 x 30.5 cm) blue construction paper for the background
- 9" (23 cm) square of orange construction paper
- 5½" (14 cm) square of yellow construction paper
- 5" (12.5 cm) square of pink construction paper
- strips of green tissue paper
- glitter
- pencil
- glue
- scissors

STEPS TO FOLLOW

1. Tear green tissue paper strips to glue to the blue construction paper.

2. Trace around the shell templates on the colors of construction paper specified.

3. Tear out the sea star.

4. Cut out the scallop and the conch shell.

5. Use glue and glitter to add details to the shells.

6. Arrange the shells and glue them to the blue paper. For an interesting effect, allow parts of the shells to extend off the paper.

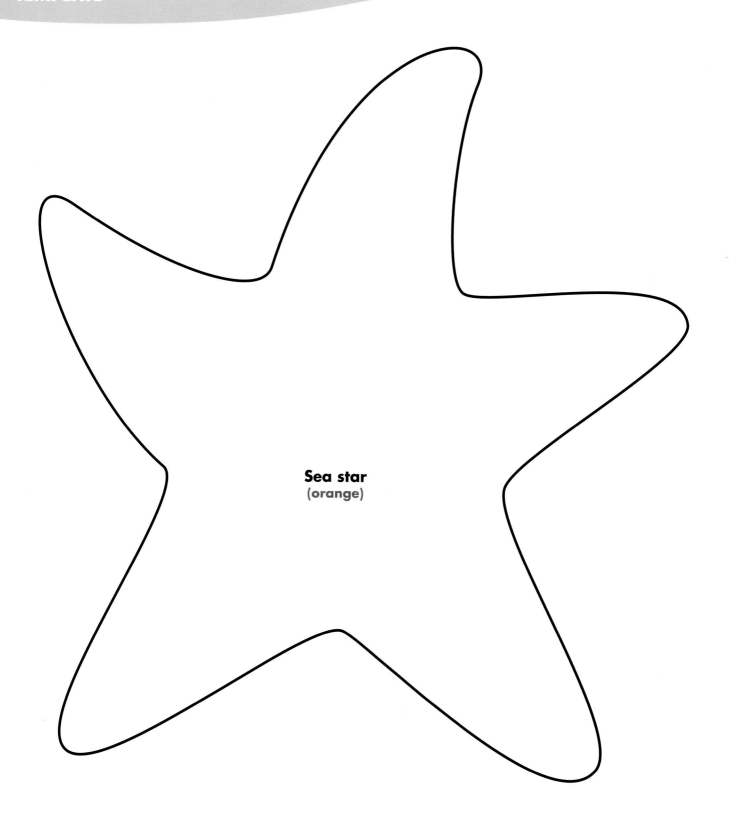

Sea star
(orange)

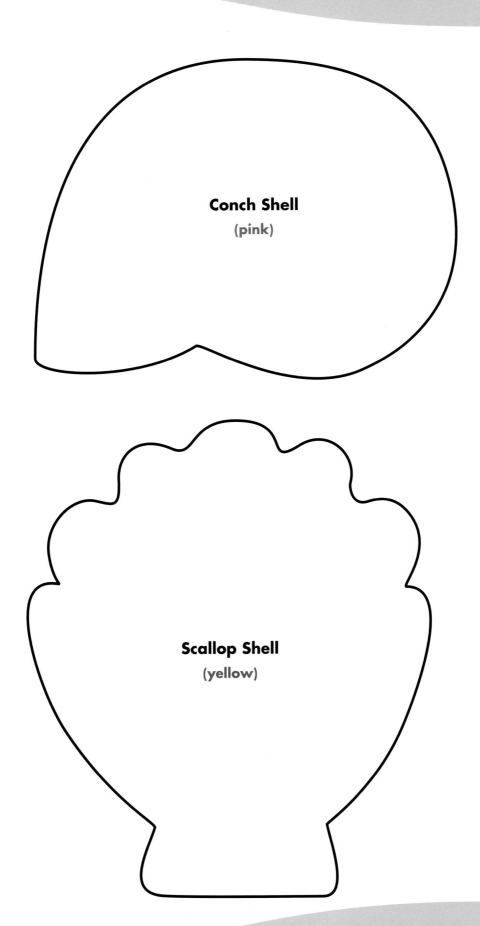

Conch Shell

(pink)

Scallop Shell

(yellow)

Seascape

STEPS TO FOLLOW

1. Cut out a circle from the orange paper.

2. Tear a rippled line along one side of the yellow paper.

3. Lay the dark blue sea, the yellow sand, and the orange sun on the light blue paper.

4. Dip the edge of the piece of cardboard in the white paint. Print white ripples on the dark blue water.

5. Color and cut out the 3 umbrellas. Experiment with stripes, polka dots, and color combinations. Make them colorful and bright.

6. Lay the black poles on the picture. Cut them to the desired lengths. Lay the umbrellas on the poles. Have students try different arrangements.

7. Glue all parts in place.

8. Add any other details with crayons, marking pens, or colored pencils.

This activity offers an opportunity to discuss different design possibilities. Encourage students to experiment with repeated shapes and colors to develop interesting variations.

MATERIALS

- patterns on the following page, reproduced for each student

- 9" x 12" (23 x 30.5 cm) light blue construction paper for the background

- 6" x 12" (15 x 30.5 cm) dark blue construction paper for the sea

- 2" x 12" (5 x 30.5 cm) yellow construction paper for the sand

- 3" (7.5 cm) square of orange construction paper for the sun

- 3—¼" x 9" (0.6 x 23 cm) black construction paper strips for the poles

- white tempera paint

- shallow dish

- strip of corrugated cardboard

- crayons, marking pens, or colored pencils

- glue

- scissors

Umbrellas

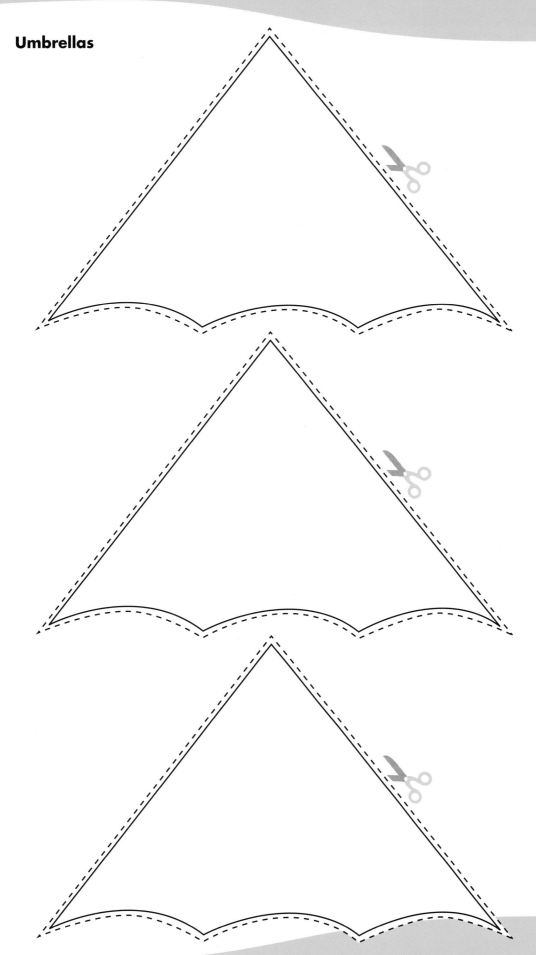

Snorkel Time

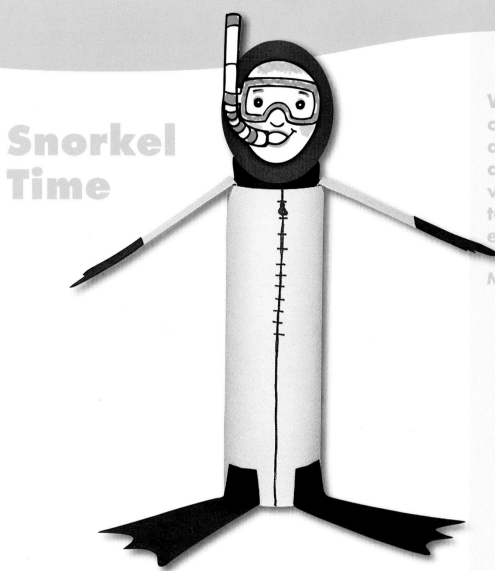

What might you see on your snorkeling adventure? This activity is a wonderful lead-in to a creative writing experience.

MATERIALS

- templates and patterns on the following page

- toilet tissue tube

- 5" x 6" (12.5 x 15 cm) yellow construction paper for the body suit

- 2—½" x 5 ½" (1.25 x 14 cm) yellow construction paper strips for the arms

- 6" (15 cm) square of black construction paper for the torso, gloves, and flippers

- scissors

- glue or tape

- crayons, marking pens, or colored pencils

STEPS TO FOLLOW

1. Draw the zipper and leg line as shown on the larger yellow paper.

2. Wrap the tube with the yellow paper. Tape or glue it in place.

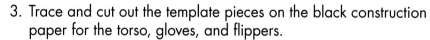

3. Trace and cut out the template pieces on the black construction paper for the torso, gloves, and flippers.

4. Fold the 2 yellow strips in half and glue a glove to one end of each arm.

5. Color and cut out the pattern for the face and snorkel. Glue it to the head.

6. Roll the torso so that it fits into the top of the tube. Also insert the arm strips on each side of the torso and bend them out and down.

7. Fold up a flap on the end of each flipper. Glue the flaps to the tube.

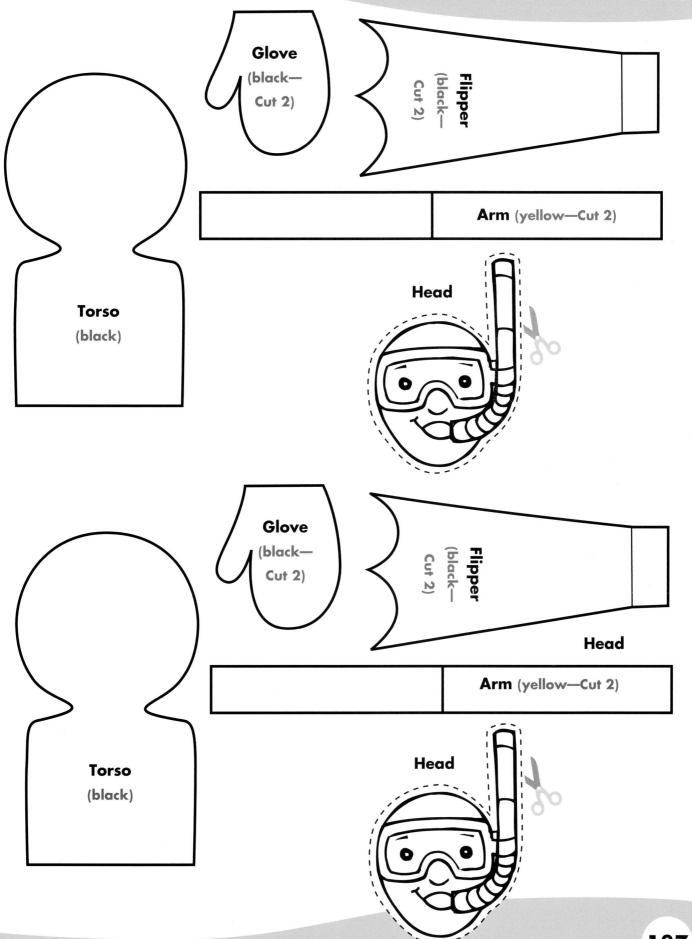

Glove
(black—
Cut 2)

Flipper
(black—
Cut 2)

Torso
(black)

Arm (yellow—Cut 2)

Head

Glove
(black—
Cut 2)

Flipper
(black—
Cut 2)

Head

Torso
(black)

Arm (yellow—Cut 2)

Head

Colorful Fish

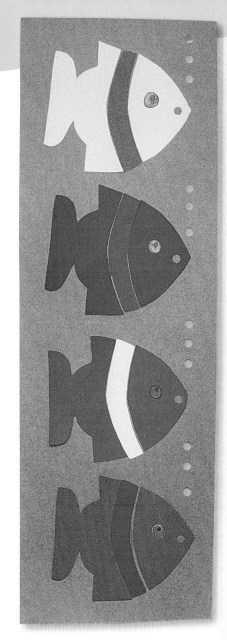

STEPS TO FOLLOW

1. Trace the fish template on each colored square of construction paper. Cut them out.

2. Color an eye for each fish.

3. Punch a hole for a mouth.

4. Draw a center stripe on the yellow fish. Hold all the fish together and cut out the stripe.

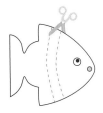

5. Lay all the fish and their parts on the blue paper. Mix and match the color stripes so that each fish has one that is a contrasting color. Glue all pieces in place.

6. Punch bubbles coming from each fish's mouth.

This easy-to-do project produces striking results that everyone will admire.

MATERIALS

- templates on the following page

- 6" x 18" (15 x 45.5 cm) dark blue construction paper for the background

- 5" (12.5 cm) squares of yellow, red, orange, and purple construction paper for the fish

- hole punch

- scissors

- glue

- crayons, marking pens, or colored pencils

- pencil

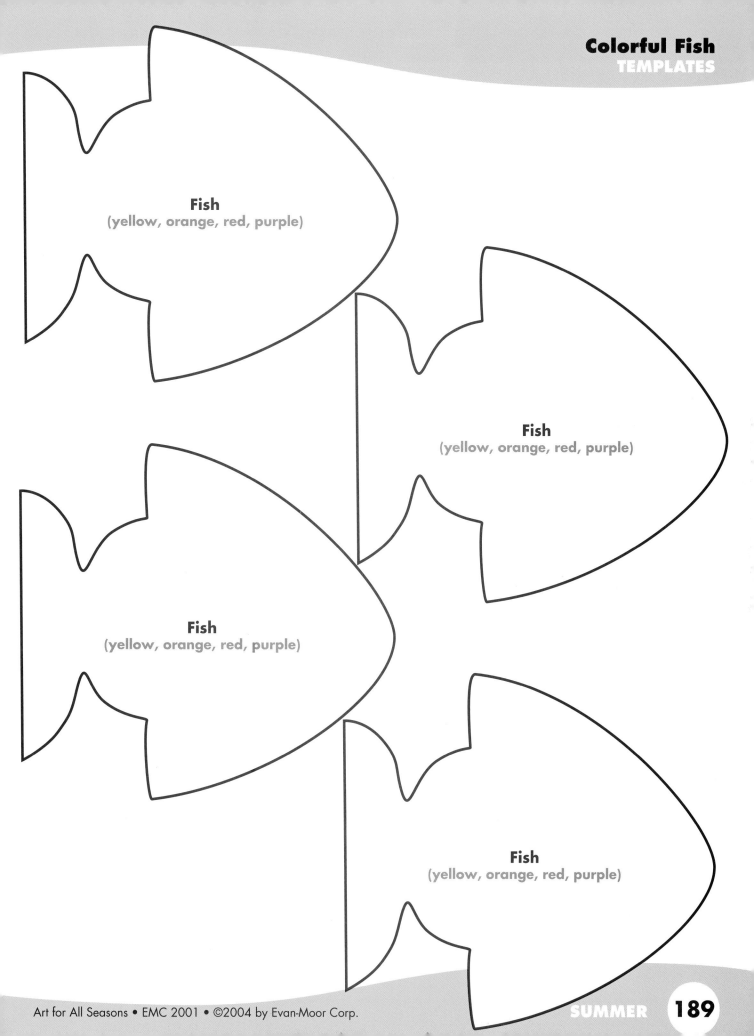

Fish
(yellow, orange, red, purple)

Fish
(yellow, orange, red, purple)

Fish
(yellow, orange, red, purple)

Fish
(yellow, orange, red, purple)

Surf's Up

STEPS TO FOLLOW

1. Dip the sponge in the white paint. Sponge paint one end of each of the blue strips of paper to create the white foam of a crashing wave. Set them aside to dry.

2. Trace around and cut out the templates for the body and the surfboard.

3. Use the construction paper provided to make hair and a swimsuit. Glue it on. Add other details with crayons, marking pens, or colored pencils.

4. Decorate the surfboard with paper scraps.

5. Fold up a flap on the feet of the surfer. Glue the flaps to the surfboard.

6. Using a pencil, curl the sponge-painted ends of the blue strips. Use double-stick tape to secure one piece of the paper to the other. Let the top sheet buckle up to resemble a wave.

7. Use double-stick tape to position the surfer on the wave.

MATERIALS

- templates on the following page
- 2—4" x 12" (10 x 30.5 cm) strips of dark blue construction paper for the water
- 2" x 5" (5 x 12.5 cm) brown construction paper for the surfboard
- 5" (12.5 cm) square of flesh-colored construction paper for the surfer
- 2" (5 cm) square of black, yellow, red, or brown construction paper for the hair
- 3" (7.5 cm) squares of various colors of construction paper for the swimsuit
- glue or double-stick tape
- scissors
- crayons, marking pens, or colored pencils
- white tempera paint
- shallow dish
- small piece of sponge
- pencil

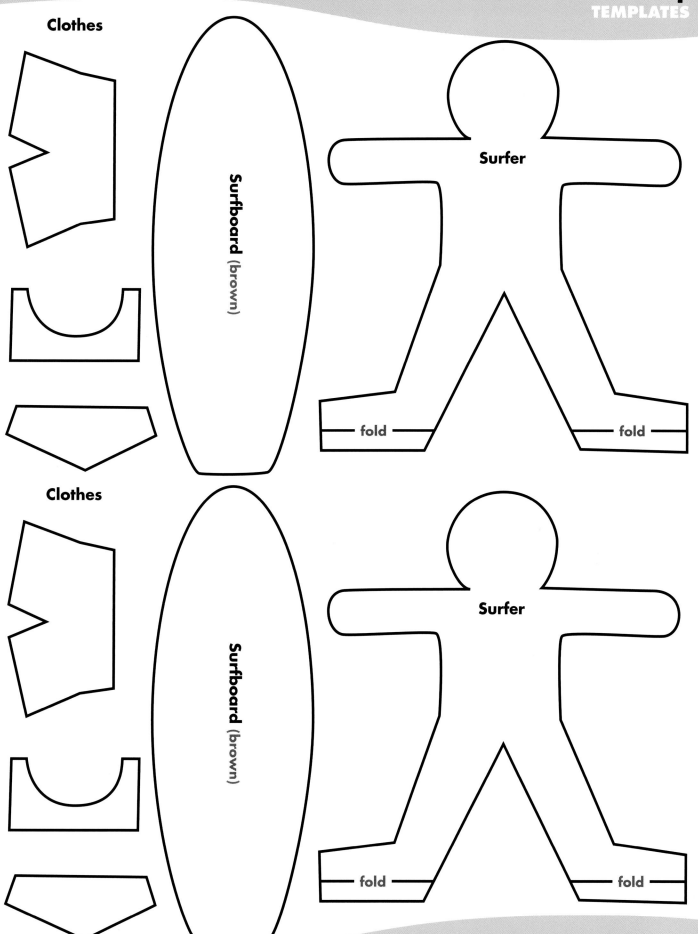

Clothes

Surfboard (brown)

Surfer

fold

fold

Clothes

Surfboard (brown)

Surfer

fold

fold

Under the Big Top

MATERIALS

- patterns and templates on the following 2 pages
- 9" x 12" (23 x 30.5 cm) yellow construction paper for the tent
- 5" x 18" (12.5 x 45.5 cm) yellow construction paper for the pull-through strip
- 9" x 12" (23 x 30.5 cm) dark blue construction paper for the tent top
- 2" x 4" (5 x 10 cm) red construction paper for the flag
- craft stick
- scissors
- glue and tape
- craft knife
- crayons, marking pens, or colored pencils

STEPS TO FOLLOW

1. Cut the 2 vertical 5" (12.5 cm) slits in the yellow tent paper as shown. Insert the pull-through strip.

2. Color and cut out the clown patterns.

3. Glue the clowns on the pull strip as you progressively pull it through the opening.

4. Color the tent top pattern. Glue it to the edge of the blue paper. Trim around the scalloped edge.

5. Fold down the top corners of the blue paper to create the peaked tent top. Glue it to the top of the yellow tent paper.

6. Using the template as a guide, cut the flag from the red paper. Glue it to the craft stick. Tape the stick to the back of the tent top.

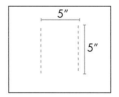

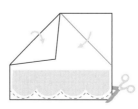

Clowns

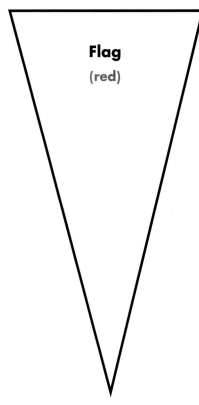

Flag
(red)

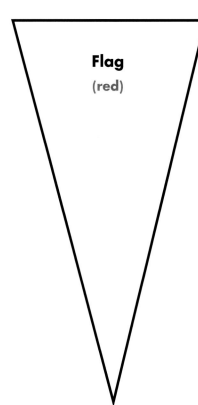

Flag
(red)

Under the Big Top

Under the Big Top

This cross-legged player can "field" a number of classroom jobs. Write the week's spelling words on the baseballs in the pocket or record the number facts students need to practice.

MATERIALS

- patterns and templates on the following page
- 9" (23 cm) square of white construction paper
- scraps of colored construction paper for the hat and mitt
- crayons, marking pens, or colored pencils
- stapler
- glue

Take Me Out to the Ball Game

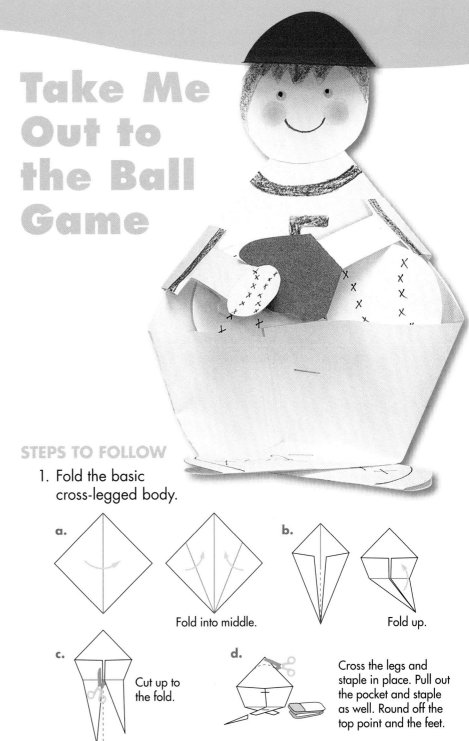

STEPS TO FOLLOW

1. Fold the basic cross-legged body.

a.

Fold into middle.

b.

Fold up.

c. Cut up to the fold.

d. Cross the legs and staple in place. Pull out the pocket and staple as well. Round off the top point and the feet.

2. Color and cut out the patterns.

3. Glue the hat to the head pattern. Glue the head to the body. Glue the mitt to the arm.

4. Color the baseball player's uniform to represent a favorite team. Show the name or initial of the team on the hat, too. Draw shoelaces and other details.

5. Fold back a flap on the top of each arm pattern. Glue the flaps to each side of the body.

6. Cut out several baseballs. Place them in the pocket.

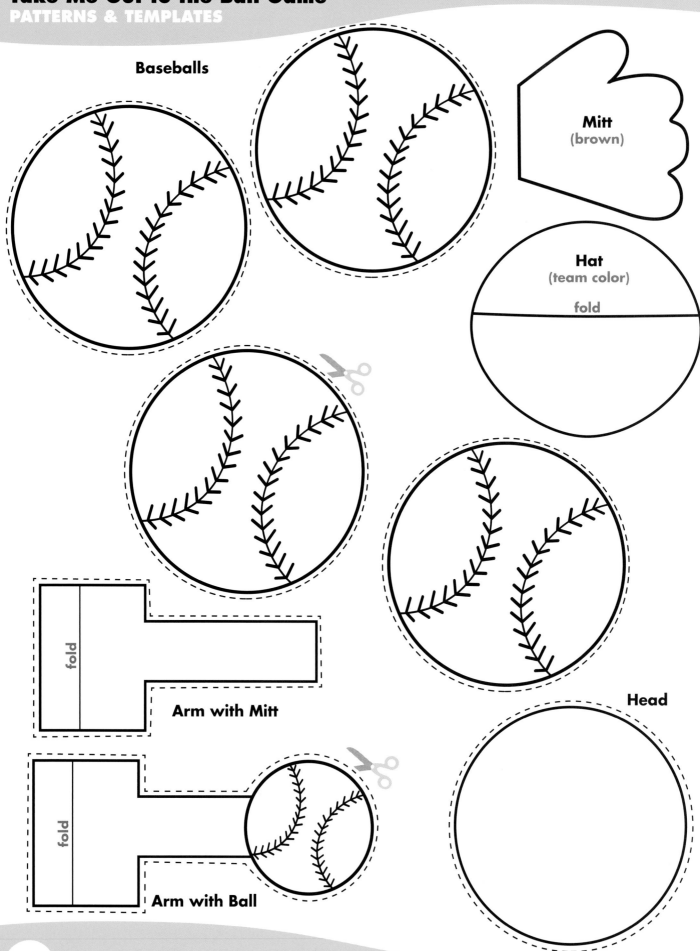

Baseballs

Mitt
(brown)

Hat
(team color)

fold

Arm with Mitt

fold

Arm with Ball

fold

Head

This project re-creates the fun of an afternoon at the park on the merry-go-round.

On the Merry-Go-Round

MATERIALS

- patterns on the following 2 pages, reproduced for each student
- 6" x 18" (15 x 45.5 cm) yellow construction paper for the merry-go-round
- 4—½" x 6" (1.25 x 15 cm) black construction paper strips for the poles
- 8" (20 cm) square of bright blue construction paper for the frame
- hole punch
- scissors
- glue
- crayons, marking pens, or colored pencils
- glitter

STEPS TO FOLLOW

1. Color and cut out the horse patterns.
2. Punch a border of holes along the top edge of the yellow strip.
3. Use glue and glitter to make a "sparkley" border along the bottom of the yellow strip.
4. Lay out the black poles on the merry-go-round, varying the heights.
5. Lay the horses on the black poles. Distribute them evenly along the strip. Glue the poles and the horses in place.
6. Roll the yellow paper into a cylinder with 1" (2.5 cm) overlap and glue to secure.
7. Color and cut out the base pattern. Glue it to the blue construction paper. Trim the blue so a border remains. Set the merry-go-round in the center of the base.

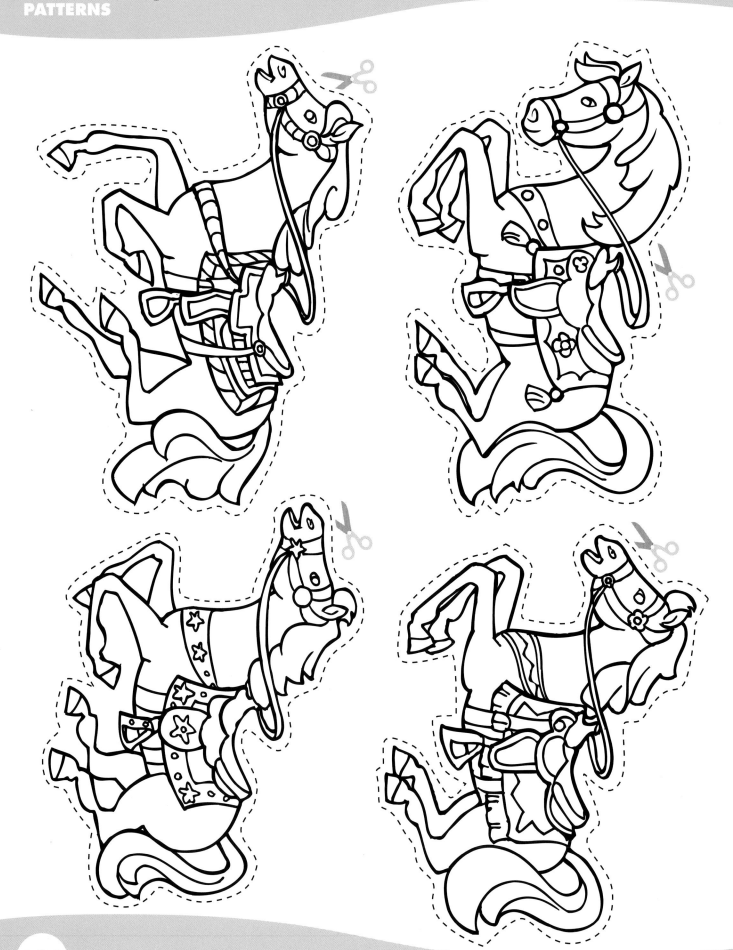

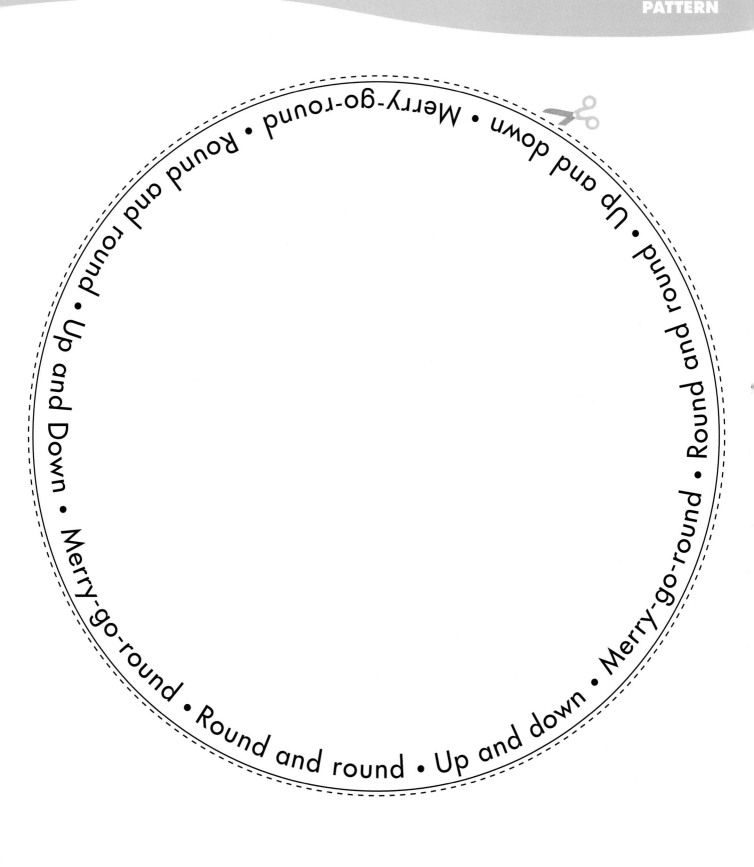

Up and Down • Merry-go-round • Round and round • Up and down • Merry-go-round • Round and round • Up and down • Merry-go-round • Round and round • Up and Down • Merry-go-round • Round and round •

Flag and Fireworks

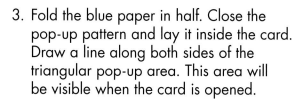

STEPS TO FOLLOW

1. Color and cut out the flag pattern.

2. Fold the pattern as shown to make the pop-up section.

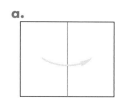 **a.**   **b.** 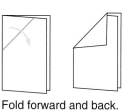   **c.**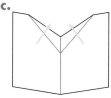

Fold forward and back.   Reverse center fold and pull forward.

3. Fold the blue paper in half. Close the pop-up pattern and lay it inside the card. Draw a line along both sides of the triangular pop-up area. This area will be visible when the card is opened.

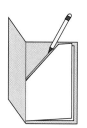

4. Apply glue and glitter in this area to give the impression of fireworks bursting.

5. Lay the folded pattern inside the card with the folds touching. Apply glue to the visible side of the pattern. Close the card and press firmly.

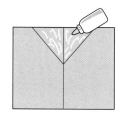

6. Flip the card over. Open the card and apply glue to the other side of the pattern. Close and press.

7. Add the red and white strips and star stickers to the front of the card.

8. Add the greeting "Happy Fourth of July."

This patriotic pop-up card is easy to make. Open and close it again and again to create the illusion of fireworks popping up behind the flag.

MATERIALS

- pattern on the following page, reproduced for each student

- 8" x 10" (20 x 25.5 cm) blue construction paper for the folder

- ¾" x 8" (2 x 20 cm) strips of red and white construction paper for the cover decoration (1 of each)

- red, gold, and silver glitter

- gold foil star stickers

- glue

- crayons, marking pens, or colored pencils

- scissors

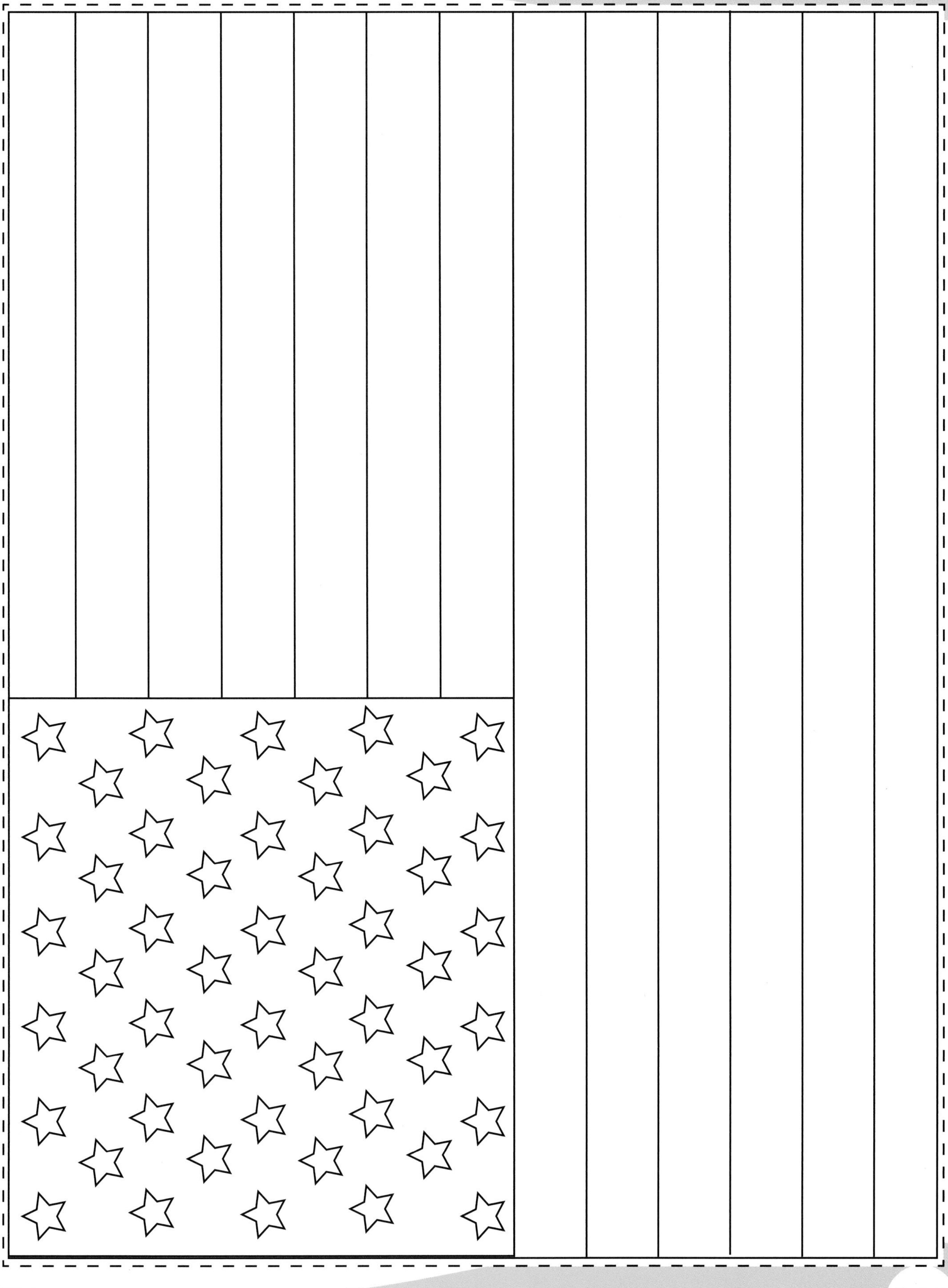

Patriotic Mobile

Cutting spirals is as much fun as seeing the finished product. This "bouncy" mobile is a colorful reminder of the 4th of July fireworks.

MATERIALS

- templates on the following 3 pages
- 7" (18 cm) squares of red, white, and blue construction paper for the spiral shapes
- 4—2" (5 cm) squares of yellow construction paper for stars
- 3 paper fasteners
- 7" (18 cm) blue paper plate
- hole punch
- scissors
- glue
- glitter
- clear plastic fishing line
- large paper clip

STEPS TO FOLLOW

1. Trace and cut out the template patterns on the red, white, and blue paper. Mark the spiral cut lines and cut. Hole punch as indicated.

2. Lay a bead of glue around each of the spiral shapes. Shake glitter onto the glue. Allow the glue to dry and then shake off the excess glitter.

3. Punch 3 holes evenly spaced on the outer edge of the paper plate. Attach one of the spiral shapes to each of these holes with a paper fastener.

4. Trace and cut out 4 yellow stars using the template as a guide. Punch a hole in the center of each one.

5. Punch 3 more holes on the edge of the paper plate. Tie an equal length of fishing line through each hole. Thread a star onto each line. Gather the lines and tie them together in a knot. Thread the last star through the combined lines. Leave a 3" (7.5 cm) length of line and tie it to the paper clip. The mobile is now ready to hang up.

Art for All Seasons • EMC 2001 • ©2004 by Evan-Moor Corp.

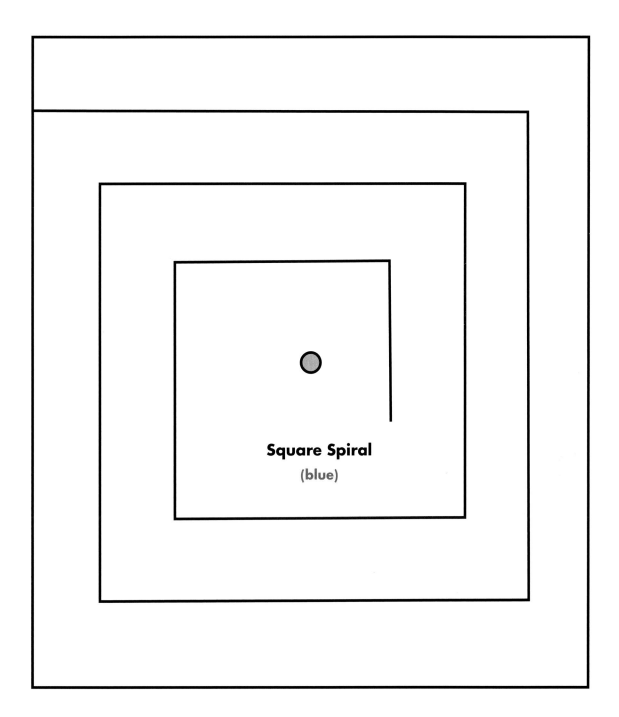

Square Spiral

(blue)

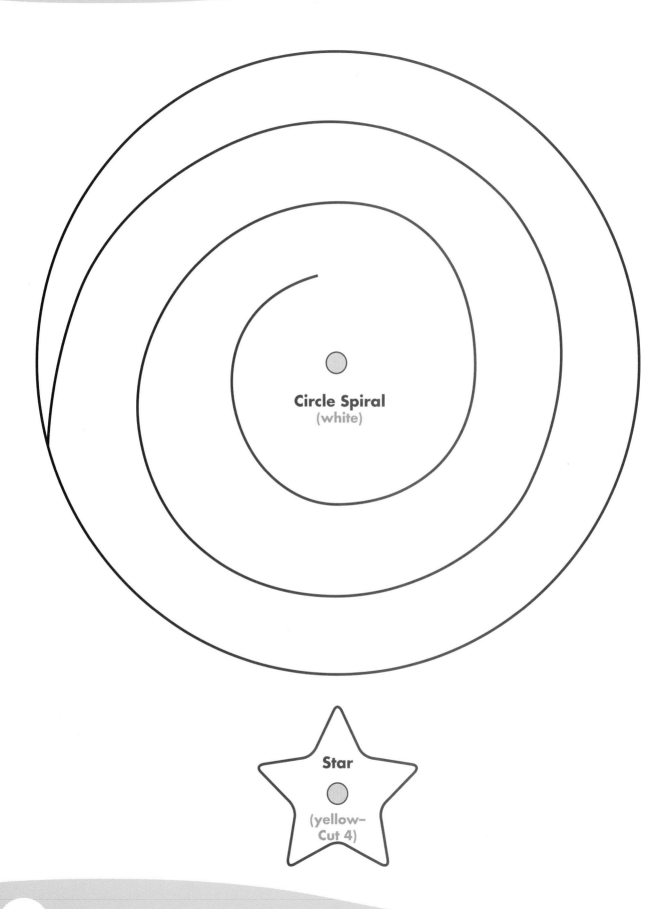

Circle Spiral
(white)

Star

(yellow–
Cut 4)

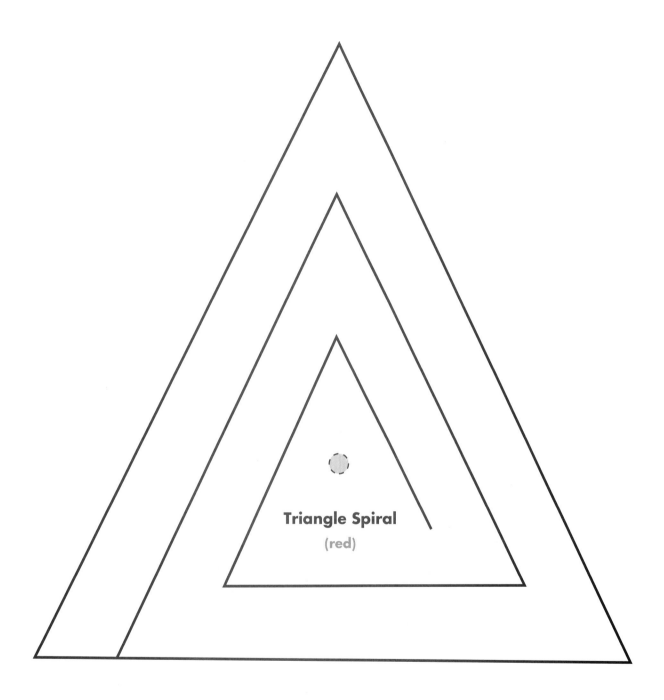

Triangle Spiral
(red)

Stars and Stripes

STEPS TO FOLLOW

1. Cut out 2 yellow and 1 blue star using the template as a guide.

2. Use the crayons, marking pens, or colored pencils to add "stars and stripes" designs to the yellow stars.

3. Tape the colored streamers to the back of one of the yellow stars.

4. Glue the stars together, designed sides facing outward, letting each one shift to show all three.

5. Punch a hole in the top point. Insert the red ribbon to create a hanger.

Hang this star-spangled streamer to add a festive spirit to your Independence Day celebration.

MATERIALS

- template on the following page
- 1" x 12" (2.5 x 30.5 cm) tissue paper strips in red, white, and blue for the streamers
- 9" (23 cm) squares of yellow and blue construction paper for the stars
- hole punch
- red foil ribbon
- crayons, marking pens, or colored pencils
- glue and tape
- scissors

Art for All Seasons • EMC 2001 • ©2004 by Evan-Moor Corp.

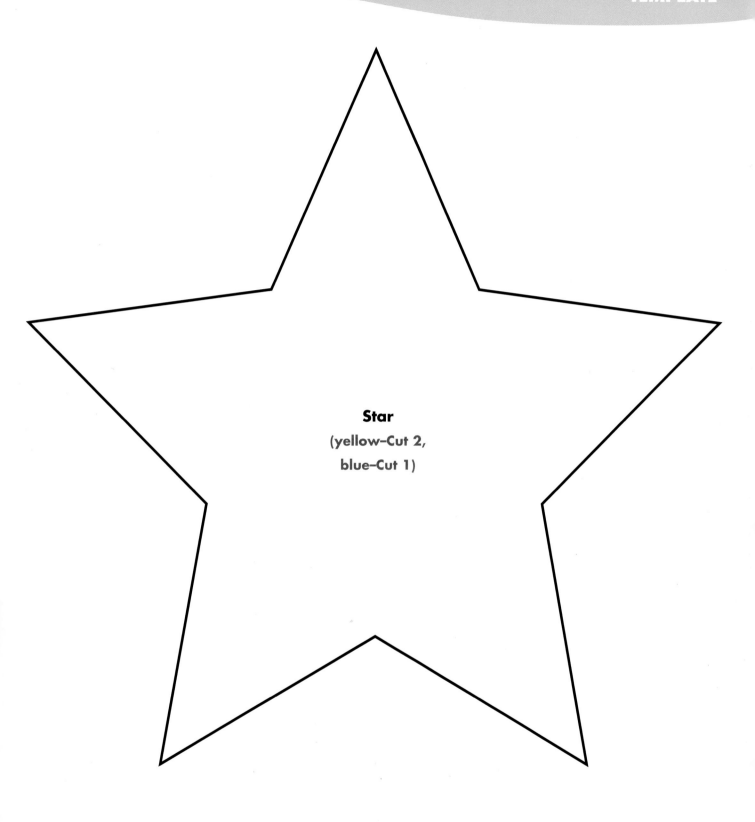

Star
(yellow–Cut 2,
blue–Cut 1)

Date: July 20

We went to a picnic today. It was at Joy and Dave's house. There was a bounce house. It was fun. I ate a hotdog, chips and a snowcone. Mommy got wet with a water balloon!

...e picnic.

This project results in a nice keepsake that highlights students' summer activities. Real photographs add interest.

Summer Memories Book

STEPS TO FOLLOW

1. Create a picture and a diary page for each memory bag in the book.

2. Glue the diary page to the bag. Glue the picture frame, with your photo, to the construction paper that slips inside the bag as shown.

3. Design one bag as the cover. Use paper scraps and crayons, marking pens, or colored pencils to create the desired effect. Use the inside front cover of the book as a table of contents.

4. Punch 2 holes on the left side of all the bags. Bind the bags together with roving. Finish it by tying a bow.

MATERIALS

- patterns on the following page, reproduced for each student

- brown paper lunch bags

- 5" x 8" (12.5 x 20 cm) colored construction paper for each bag in the book

- construction paper scraps

- roving or yarn

- scissors

- glue

- hole punch

- crayons, marking pens, or colored pencils